Interactive Notebooks

SEASONAL

Grade 1

Credits

Authors: Angela Triplett, Melissa Parthemore
Copy Editor: Elise Craver

Visit *carsondellosa.com* for correlations to Common Core, state, national, and Canadian provincial standards.

Carson-Dellosa Publishing LLC
PO Box 35665
Greensboro, NC 27425 USA
carsondellosa.com

ISBN 978-1-4838-5025-2
01-305187784

Table of Contents

*This lesson includes multiple reproducible pages. It is designed to introduce one or more concepts at a time, and can be taught over time. Once assembled, it will use multiple pages in a student's interactive notebook or create more complex pages with more pieces.

What Are Interactive Notebooks?

Interactive notebooks are a unique form of note taking. Teachers guide students through creating pages of notes on new topics. Instead of being in the traditional linear, handwritten format, notes are colorful and spread across the pages. Notes also often include drawings, diagrams, and 3-D elements to make the material understandable and relevant. Students are encouraged to complete their notebook pages in ways that make sense to them. With this personalization, no two pages are exactly the same.

Whether you are new to interactive notebooks, or already use interactive notebooks in one or more subject areas, seasonal templates are the perfect addition to any curriculum. New seasons and holidays always hold excitement for students—take advantage of that natural engagement and give students opportunities to practice essential skills in an appealing context. Interactive notebooks make it easy to provide hands-on activities to support, teach, and review during different seasons and holidays throughout the year.

Because of their creative nature, interactive notebooks allow students to be active participants in their own learning. Using seasonally appropriate templates all year long is a fun way to engage students in skill practice and review. For more information on how to integrate seasonal interactive notebooks into your daily and weekly plans, see page 5.

For interactive templates to introduce skills and concepts in math, language arts, word study, and science, pick up the other grade-level books in the Interactive Notebook series.

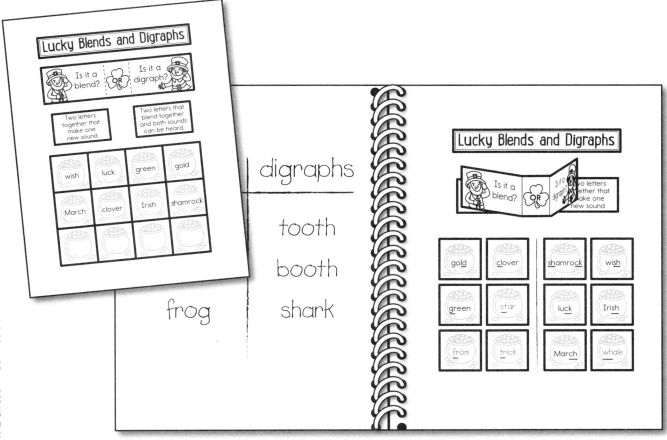

A student's interactive notebook for blends and digraphs

Traditional vs. Seasonal Interactive Notebooks

In many ways, seasonal interactive notebook pages are like traditional interactive notebook pages. However, they are different in several essential ways. Once you understand the similarities and differences between the two types, you can decide how seasonal interactive notebooks will best fit into your schedule and curriculum.

Traditional Interactive Notebooks

- primarily for learning and understanding new skills
- focus on one subject area
- one notebook per subject area
- often created during a whole-group lesson

Both

- fun and engaging
- standards-based
- hands-on learning
- use interactive elements like flaps and pockets
- often include personal connections to content

Seasonal Interactive Notebooks

- primarily for practicing and reviewing skills
- include a variety of subject areas
- may be placed in different notebooks based on subject or stand-alone pages
- can often be created independently

Note about the Autumn Templates

Because autumn is typically the beginning of the school year, the focus of those early weeks is often on reviewing essential skills from the previous grade. So, the interactive templates provided for autumn will include activities that review concepts that are considered below the current grade level. That way, they can be used immediately and will help to ensure students are starting off with last year's concepts solidly in place before you begin to teach new skills and concepts.

How to Use Seasonal Interactive Notebooks

Use the seasonal templates as a time-saving way to incorporate festive fun and excitement in the classroom. This series is a great resource for adding a seasonal element to your math, reading, science, and social studies curriculums. Due to their slightly different nature (see page 4), seasonal templates may work better for your classroom needs by placing them in their own single-subject notebooks, within your existing notebooks, or as stand-alone "lapbooks." Choose the option that works best for your classroom.

Using Traditional Notebooks

Interactive notebooks are usually either single-subject, spiral-bound notebooks, composition books, or three-ring binders with loose-leaf paper. Create a separate seasonal interactive notebook using any of these types. Simply create a table of contents marked with each month and the seasons and holidays that correspond with that month. Place the corresponding templates inside.

Using Existing Interactive Notebooks

Seasonal interactive notebook pages can be used to supplement your students' existing language arts, math, science, or social studies notebooks. Add each template to the subject notebook near the original pages relating to the skill that is being practiced, or add them to the next blank page. For example, if the seasonal notebook page deals with blends and digraphs, have students complete the page in their language arts interactive notebooks.

Using Lapbooks

A lapbook is a file folder that has been folded in a certain manner to accommodate one or more interactive notebook page activities (see diagram below). Lapbooks generally include more information and more hands-on activities relating to a single subject than a typical notebook page. So, students might create a single lapbook about symmetry that includes standard teaching interactive templates as well as the related seasonal template. You may choose to create in-depth subject lapbooks with several different templates and hands-on activities, or create a single seasonal template within a lapbook so it can stand alone.

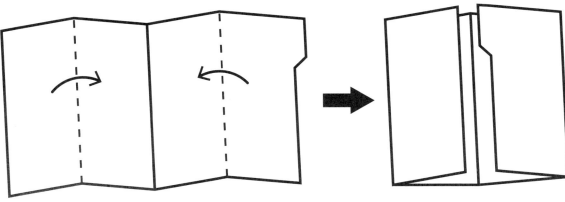

Fold the sides in toward the center.

Managing Seasonal Interactive Notebooks

Make It Independent

- Create a model page for students to refer to. Use it for absent students or place it in a center. Or, place it in a prominent place in the classroom for students to refer to if they don't finish on time.

- As you create the model page, take photos of each step. Use presentation or word document software to show the photos in order, labeled step-by-step (depending on your students' reading levels). Print a copy to keep in the model notebook or post in a center.

Make It Festive

- Instead of copying templates on white paper, use paper in seasonal colors to add a spot of festive color.

- Allow students to use seasonal stickers and other flat decorative objects to complete each page. For example, if students are required to draw a set under a flap, let students place seasonal stickers under the flap instead of drawing. Or, if students are tasked with coming up with a noun, verb, and adjective to describe an object, give them seasonal stickers to place on their pages and have them record the related parts of speech that describe each sticker.

Creating Notebook Pages

- For storing loose pieces, add a pocket to the inside back cover. Use an envelope, a jumbo library pocket, or a resealable plastic bag. Or, tape the bottom and side edges of the two last pages of the notebook together to create a large pocket.

- When writing under flaps, have students trace the outline of each flap so they can visualize the writing boundary.

- Where the dashed line will be hidden on the inside of a fold, have students first fold the piece in the opposite direction so they can see the dashed line. Then, students should fold the piece back the other way along the same fold line to create the fold in the correct direction.

- To avoid losing pieces, have students keep all of their scraps on their desks until they have finished each page.

- To contain paper scraps and avoid multiple trips to the trash can, provide small groups with small buckets or tubs.

- For students who run out of room, keep full and half sheets available. Students can glue these to the bottom of those pages and fold them up when not in use.

Accountability with Interactive Notebooks

As with any other classroom work, students need to be held accountable for their work in interactive notebooks. This will ensure they are doing their best work and that the information included is accurate and will serve as a valuable, error-free resource.

Set Clear Expectations

From the beginning, make sure students know what you expect an interactive notebook page to look like. Use the following questions to outline your expectations.

- What should the edges of the pieces look like after they've been cut out?
- Does it matter if all of the pieces are in the same spot as everyone else's?
- How will the pieces be adhered to the page?
- Can students use pens, colored pencils, markers, etc.?
- What does a neat notebook page look like?
- Should every page have a title? The date?
- How and when should missed pages be completed?
- Where will the notebooks be stored?
- When can students access their notebooks?
- Will students be able to take their notebooks home?

Then, communicate those expectations with one or more of the following:

- Create an anchor chart with students, outlining the expectations.
- Have students glue expectations sheets or rubrics (see pages 8 and 9) to the inside front covers of their notebooks.
- Model, model, model! Create notebook pages along with students so they have a clear vision of what an ideal page looks like.
- Have students sign an interactive notebooks contract to indicate they know the expectations and will follow them.

Have Students Evaluate Themselves

Provide students with copies of the Interactive Notebook Reflection (page 8) so they can assess their own work and reflect on what they did well and what they can improve on. You may then choose to assess the notebook page with the same reflection worksheet and compare the reflections to hold students accountable.

Assess the Notebooks

Don't feel that you have to assess every page. Choose an interval and stick to that. Will you assess every page? Once a week? A month? A quarter? Randomly? It can be time-consuming to do an entire class's worth at once, so do four to six at a time. Use the Grading Rubric (page 9) to clearly and consistently assess students' work.

Interactive Notebook Reflection

Page Title _____   Page Number _____

I cut neatly.

I colored inside the lines.

I used just the right amount of glue.

I used neat handwriting.

The page is complete and correct.

Color the stars to show the rating you would give your page.

Interactive Notebook Grading Rubric

4

_____ Table of contents is complete.

_____ All notebook pages are included.

_____ All notebook pages are complete.

_____ Notebook pages are neat and organized.

_____ Information is correct.

_____ Pages show personalization, evidence of learning, and original ideas.

3

_____ Table of contents is mostly complete.

_____ One notebook page is missing.

_____ Notebook pages are mostly complete.

_____ Notebook pages are mostly neat and organized.

_____ Information is mostly correct.

_____ Pages show some personalization, evidence of learning, and original ideas.

2

_____ Table of contents is missing a few entries.

_____ A few notebook pages are missing.

_____ A few notebook pages are incomplete.

_____ Notebook pages are somewhat messy and unorganized.

_____ Information has several errors.

_____ Pages show little personalization, evidence of learning, or original ideas.

1

_____ Table of contents is incomplete.

_____ Many notebook pages are missing.

_____ Many notebook pages are incomplete.

_____ Notebook pages are too messy and unorganized to use.

_____ Information is incorrect.

_____ Pages show no personalization, evidence of learning, or original ideas.

Apple Addition with Ten Frames

Introduction

Remind students that a good strategy to use when adding within 10 is to draw and use a ten frame. Distribute index cards to each student. Students should draw a ten frame on their cards. Using a red crayon or dot marker, have students draw between 1 and 8 dots on their ten frames. Then, have students exchange cards with a partner. The partner should fill in any number of the remaining blank sections of the ten frame with a yellow crayon or dot marker. On the back of the index card, each student should write an addition sentence that corresponds with the ten frame representation shown.

Creating the Notebook Page

Guide students through the following steps to complete the right-hand page in their notebooks.

1. Add a Table of Contents entry for the Apple Addition with Ten Frames pages.

2. Cut out the title and glue it to the top of the page.

3. Cut out the ten frame flaps. Apply glue to the backs of the top sections and attach them to the page.

4. Cut out the apple pieces.

5. Count the apples on each flap. Glue any number of apple pieces onto the remaining spaces on each ten frame to create an addition problem. Write the number sentence on the top of the flap.

6. Write or draw the new number under each flap.

Reflect on Learning

To complete the left-hand page, have each student draw a ten frame. Write an addition sentence on the board such as *4 + 3 = ?*. Students should use red and yellow crayons or markers to represent the addition sentences on their ten frame and find the sum.

© Carson-Dellosa • CD-105014

Apple Addition

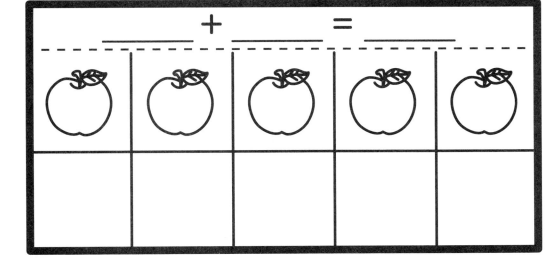

____ + ____ = ____

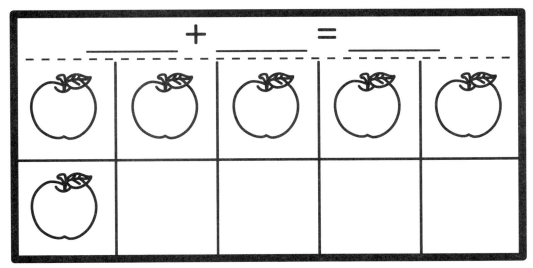

____ + ____ = ____

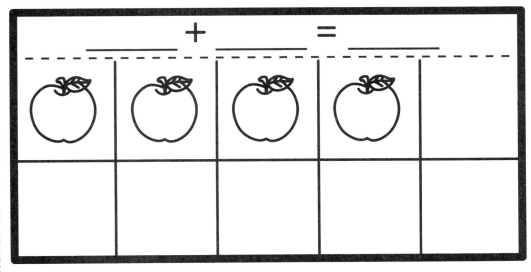

____ + ____ = ____

Apple Addition with Ten Frames

The Apple Man: Character Traits

Introduction

Read a book or watch a video about Johnny Appleseed. Discuss how Johnny Appleseed is called a folk hero because of how he planted many apple trees and helped farmers grow apple orchards. Then, review the definition of character traits as *adjectives used to describe someone's personality.* Discuss how character traits can be good or bad. Say character traits such as *hard worker, kind, lazy,* etc. If students think the character trait describes Johnny Appleseed students should raise their right hands. If they think the character trait does not, then students should raise their left hands. Have students discuss why the character trait describes Johnny Appleseed.

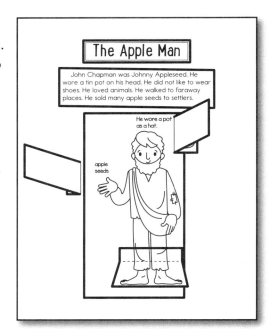

Creating the Notebook Page

Guide students through the following steps to complete the right-hand page in their notebooks.

1. Add a Table of Contents entry for The Apple Man: Character Traits pages.

2. Cut out the title and glue it to the top of the page.

3. Cut out the story piece and glue it to the page below the title.

4. Cut out the Johnny Appleseed piece and glue it to the center of the page.

5. Read the story of Johnny Appleseed together.

6. Cut out the flaps. Apply glue to the backs of the narrow sections and attach them to the Johnny Appleseed piece, gluing the tin pot flap on his head, the *What did he sell?* piece over his hand, and the bare feet piece on the bottom of his legs.

7. Under the tin pot hat flap and the bare feet flap, write two character traits that describe Johnny Appleseed. On the *What did he sell?* flap, draw an apple. Under the flap, write the answer to the question.

Reflect on Learning

To complete the left-hand page, brainstorm several positive character traits such as *helpful, nice, smart,* etc. and write them on the board. Have students draw a stick figure version of Johnny Appleseed. Then, students should use the words on the board to describe the character traits of Johnny Appleseed by writing them around the stick figure drawing.

The Apple Man

John Chapman was Johnny Appleseed. He wore a tin pot on his head. He did not like to wear shoes. He loved animals. He walked to faraway places. He sold many apple seeds to settlers.

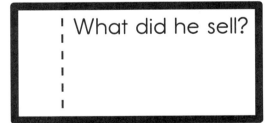

What did he sell?

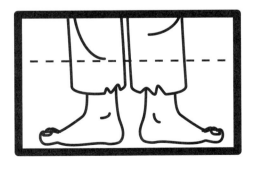

Columbus Day Sight Words

Introduction

Review the sight words *are, day, is, an, in,* and *going* by drawing sailboats on the board and writing a sight word in each one of the boats. Have the class read the words as you point to each boat. Then, post boats around the room with different sight words from the lesson written on each one of the boats. Students should walk around to each boat and read the sight word with partners.

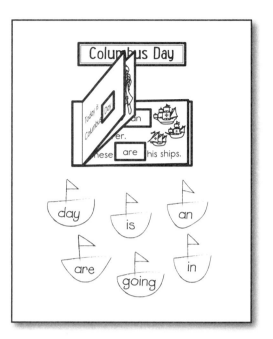

Creating the Notebook Page

Guide students through the following steps to complete the right-hand page in their notebooks.

1. Add a Table of Contents entry for the Columbus Day Sight Words pages.

2. Cut out the title and glue it to the top of the page.

3. Cut out the four pages of the book. Sequence the story in order from beginning to end.

4. Cut out the word cards.

5. Read the story about Christopher Columbus. Glue each word card onto the correct box.

6. Apply glue to the gray glue sections and stack the flaps on top of each other in order to create a four-page stacked flap book.

7. Apply glue to the back of the last page and attach it to the page below the title.

8. Read the story again with a partner.

9. Copy each of the sight words below the book. Draw a boat around each sight word.

Reflect on Learning

To complete the left-hand page, have students write short sentences using the sight words *are, day, is, an, in,* and *going.*

Columbus Day

Word Box
are
Day
going
is
an
in

Today is Columbus [glue] .

This [glue] Christopher Columbus.

He was [glue] explorer. These [glue] his ships.

He was [glue] to India. He landed [glue] America.

Candy Corn Making Ten

Have four volunteers stand in a line at the front of the room. Ask students how many more volunteers would need to come to the front of the room to have 10 students standing altogether. Call on one additional volunteer at a time to stand with the others. Count on aloud as each volunteer adds to the line until 10 is reached. Ask students again how many more students were needed to reach 10 students (6). Repeat the activity several more times with different starting amounts for extra practice.

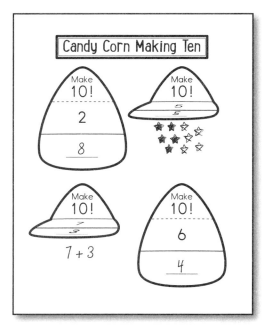

Creating the Notebook Page

Guide students through the following steps to complete the right-hand page in their notebooks.

1. Add a Table of Contents entry for the Candy Corn Making Ten pages.

2. Cut out the title and glue it to the top of the page.

3. Cut out the candy corn pieces. Apply glue to the backs of the top sections and attach them to the page.

4. Look at the number in the center of each candy corn. Decide what number is needed to make ten. Write it in the bottom section of each candy corn.

5. Write a number sentence or draw a picture to represent the numbers under each flap.

Reflect on Learning

To complete the left-hand page, have students draw and color a rainbow with six arcs. Label the first six arcs on the left side 0–5 at the bottom of each arc. Students should figure out the number that would make ten on the other side of the matching arc and write it below the arc on the right side. What do students notice?

Candy Corn Making Ten

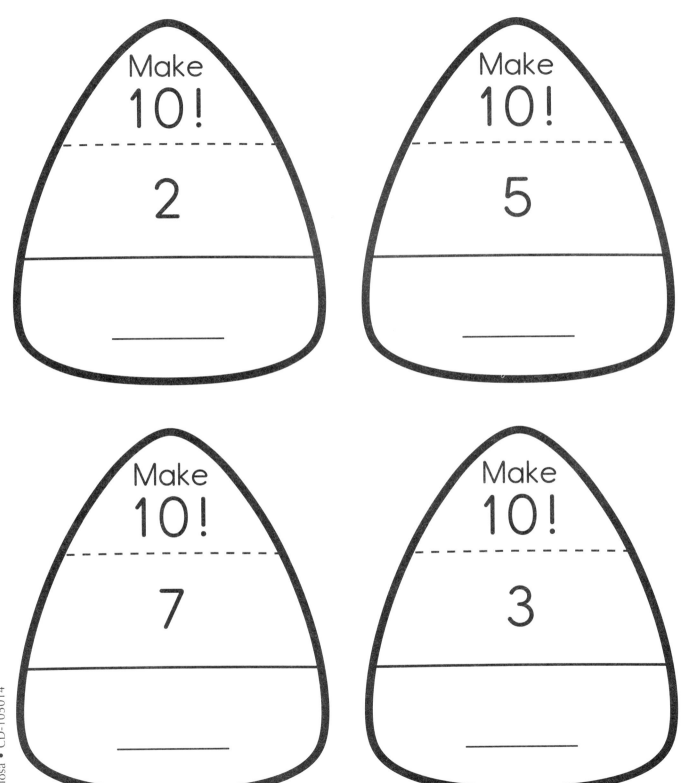

Make
10!
2
____

Make
10!
5
____

Make
10!
7
____

Make
10!
3
____

Fact and Opinion Pumpkin Patch

Introduction

Explain to students the difference between a fact and an opinion. Discuss how a fact is something that can be proven to be true. An opinion is something a person thinks or feels. Label each side of the room *fact* and *opinion*. Then, say several different fact and opinion statements such as *pumpkins are ugly* or *pumpkins grow on vines*. Have students decide if each statement is a fact or an opinion, then walk to the appropriate side of the room. Discuss why each statement is a fact or an opinion.

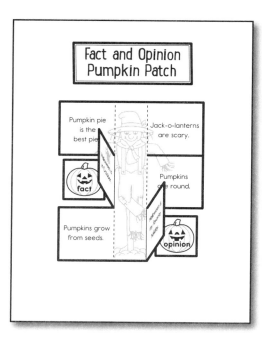

Creating the Notebook Page

Guide students through the following steps to complete the right-hand page in their notebooks.

1. Add a Table of Contents entry for the Fact and Opinion Pumpkin Patch pages.

2. Cut out the title and glue it to the top of the page.

3. Cut out the flap book. Cut on the solid lines to create six flaps. Apply glue to the back of the middle section and attach it to the page.

4. Read the sentences on the flaps and decide which ones are facts and which ones are opinions.

5. Cut out the *fact* and *opinion* pumpkin pieces. Glue them under the corresponding flaps.

Reflect on Learning

To complete the left-hand page, have students take turns saying fact and opinion statements with partners. Each partner should say if the statement is a fact or opinion. Have them write or draw the facts and opinions and label them *F* for fact or *O* for opinion.

Fact and Opinion Pumpkin Patch

Pumpkin pie is the best pie.

Jack-o-lanterns are scary.

Halloween is in October.

Pumpkins are round.

Pumpkins grow from seeds.

Halloween is my favorite holiday.

Web of Fact Fluency

Introduction

Discuss why memorizing math facts is important and can help students solve problems quickly and accurately. Then, place one flash card on each desk. Have students stand behind or beside the desk. On the teacher's word, students have a set (short) amount of time to find the answer and flip to check. Then, say *Scoot!* and students will move to the next desk and repeat.

Creating the Notebook Page

Guide students through the following steps to complete the right-hand page in their notebooks.

1. Add a Table of Contents entry for the Web of Fact Fluency pages.

2. Cut out the title and glue it to the top of the page.

3. Cut out the pockets. Apply glue to the backs of the three tabs and attach the pockets to the page. It may be helpful to fold on the dashed lines to create visual borders before applying the glue.

4. Cut out the problem cards.

5. Quickly solve the addition or subtraction problem on each card and sort them into the correct pockets. If there are facts you cannot answer yet, put them in the *I'm Stuck!* pocket and return to them later.

Reflect on Learning

To complete the left-hand page, have students number their pages 1–10. Display ten different flash cards. Students should write the answers to each flash card problem in their notebooks.

Web of Fact Fluency

+	−	? I'm Stuck!

2 + 2	5 + 1	7 − 2	3 + 3	6 − 2
4 − 1	9 − 8	5 + 3	7 + 2	4 + 2
9 − 3	1 + 3	8 + 1	6 + 3	8 − 5

Election Day Graphing

Introduction

Review the terms *candidate*, *nominate*, *election*, and *vote*. Relate the vocabulary words to the presidential election. Then, hold a mock election. Have students nominate the names of specialists in their school for the *Best Specialist Award*. Students should be able to explain the qualities of their candidate that would make them the best nominee. Each student should write their choice on a slip of paper. Provide a shoe box as a ballot box. Tally the votes and create a bar graph to show the results of the election.

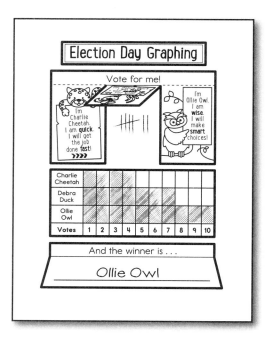

Creating the Notebook Page

Guide students through the following steps to complete the right-hand page in their notebooks.

1. Add a Table of Contents entry for the Election Day Graphing pages.

2. Cut out the title and glue it to the top of the page.

3. Cut out the *Vote for me!* flap book. Cut on the solid lines to create three flaps. Apply glue to the back of the top section and attach it to the page below the title.

4. Cut out the graph piece. Glue it to the page below the *Vote for me!* piece.

5. Cut out the *And the winner is . . .* flap. Apply glue to the back of the top section and attach it to the bottom of the page.

6. Read each candidate's sign. Collect tally votes in the *Vote for me!* flap book by asking your classmates who they would like to vote for. Tally the votes under the matching flaps.

7. Count the tallies and use the data to complete the graph.

8. Write the name of the animal with the most votes on the *And the winner is . . .* flap. Under the flap, explain how you know who won the election.

Reflect on Learning

To complete the left-hand page, tell students that you are thinking of taking them on a field trip and you are trying to decide between the zoo, the museum, or the park. Write the three choices on the board. Give each student a slip of paper. She should write her choice of field trip on the paper and put it into the ballot box used in the introduction lesson. Tally the results as a class and write them on the board. Students should create bar graphs to represent the data collected.

Election Day Graphing

Vote for me!

I'm Charlie Cheetah. I am **quick**. I will get the job done **fast!** >>>>

I'm Debra Duck. I am **loud**. I will **speak up** for you!

I'm Ollie Owl. I am **wise**. I will make **smart** choices!

Charlie Cheetah										
Debra Duck										
Ollie Owl										
Votes	1	2	3	4	5	6	7	8	9	10

And the winner is . . .

_____

Fact Family Feathers

Introduction

Review how a fact family is made of the two or four related addition and subtraction facts between three numbers. For example, *1 + 3 = 4, 3 + 1 = 4, 4 − 3 = 1,* and *4 − 1 = 3* make up a fact family. Then, distribute a domino to each student. (Do not include dominoes with zero, doubles, or sums over 10.) Have each student use the two numbers represented on her domino to create and record a fact family. Repeat the activity for additional practice.

Creating the Notebook Page

Guide students through the following steps to complete the right-hand page in their notebooks.

1. Add a Table of Contents entry for the Fact Family Feathers pages.

2. Cut out the title and glue it to the top of the page.

3. Cut out the turkey piece with the numbers. Apply glue to the back of the middle part of the turkey body and attach it to the page. Leave enough space around the turkey to attach the feathers.

4. Cut out the feather pieces with numbers. Look at the numbers on the turkey piece. Use the numbers to fill in the boxes with the missing numbers and complete the fact family. Glue the feathers around the turkey piece.

5. Repeat steps 3–4 with the blank turkey and feather pieces. Fill in a fact family of your choosing.

Reflect on Learning

To complete the left-hand page, have each student draw an outline of their hand (without the thumb) to create a turkey with four feathers. Write three numbers on the board such as *7, 4,* and *3.* Have students copy the numbers in the palm of the drawn hand. Then, students should write the fact family of those numbers in the fingers of their drawings.

Fact Family Feathers

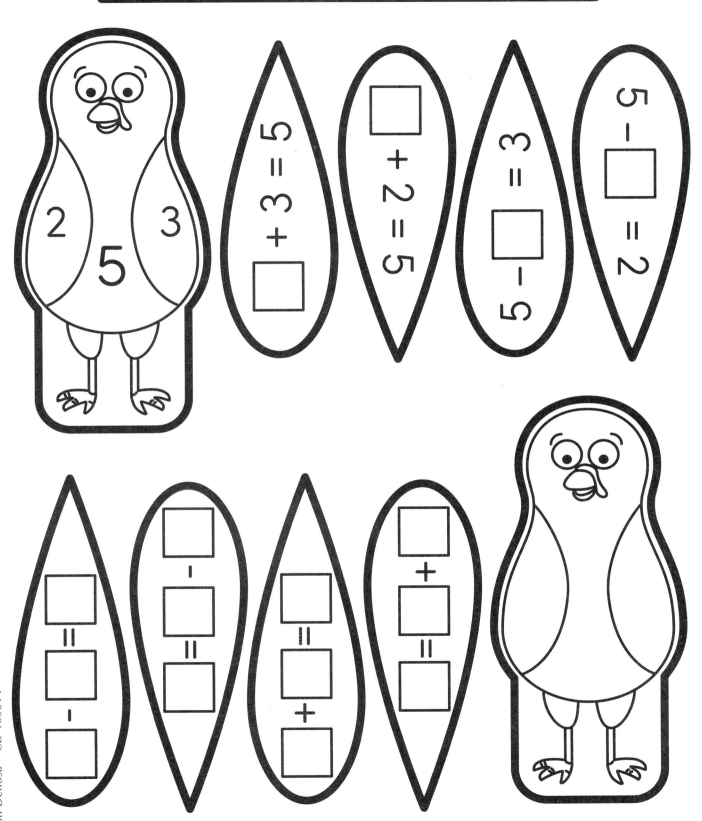

Penguin body with: 2 3 5

Feathers:
- 5 + 3 = □
- □ + 2 = 5
- 3 = □ − 5
- 5 − □ = 2
- □ − □ = □
- □ − □ = □
- □ = □ + □
- □ + □ = □

Thanksgiving Then and Now

Introduction

Program two corners of the room to represent *Then* and *Now* by posting pictures of historical objects such as old model cars or antique items and items that presently exist such as flat screen TVs into the corresponding corners. Discuss the pictures and why they are labeled *Then* or *Now*. Next, show additional pictures of past and present objects. For each picture shown, have students walk to the correct corner of the room. Finally, discuss some of the items the Pilgrims and Native American Indians may have used or worn and how they are different from what is used or worn today.

Creating the Notebook Page

Guide students through the following steps to complete the right-hand page in their notebooks.

1. Add a Table of Contents entry for the Thanksgiving Then and Now pages.

2. Cut out the title and glue it to the top of the page.

3. Cut out the story piece and glue it to the page below the title.

4. Cut out the pockets. Apply glue to the backs of the three tabs and attach the pockets to the page. It may be helpful to fold on the dashed lines to create visual borders before applying the glue.

5. Cut out the picture cards.

6. Read about the similarities and differences between Pilgrim children and present-day children. Decide whether the picture on each card represents a Pilgrim child or a present-day child. Sort the cards into the correct pockets.

Reflect on Learning

To complete the left-hand page, have students draw a line to divide their notebook pages in half. Label the halves *Then* and *Now*. Students should think of objects they had as younger children such as baby bottles and draw them in the *Then* column. Students should think of objects they currently own and draw them in the *Now* column.

Thanksgiving Then and Now

Did you know you and Pilgrim children have a lot in common? Pilgrim children lived in log homes. They did chores. They played games. They wore shoes and hats. They used candles for lights. Pilgrim children went to school but they did not have computers. They did not go on field trips. Their life was a little different from yours today!

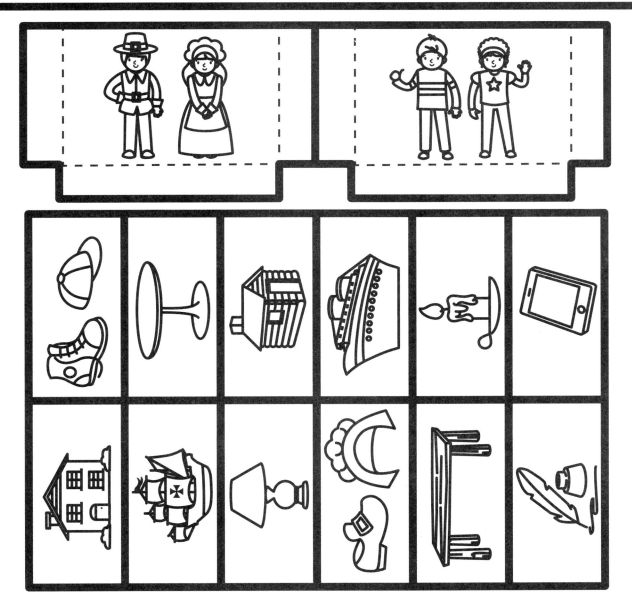

Animals in Winter

Introduction

Introduce the words *migrate* (to move), *hibernate* (to sleep), and *adapt* (to change). Discuss animals, such as butterflies who migrate, bears who hibernate, and snowshoe rabbits who adapt and change their fur color to blend in with a snowy environment. Then, have students partner together and act out the meaning of all three words.

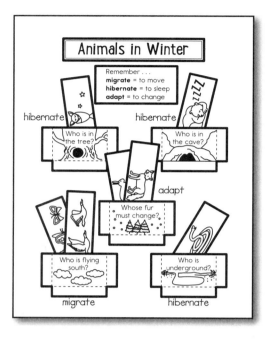

Creating the Notebook Page

Guide students through the following steps to complete the right-hand page in their notebooks.

1. Add a Table of Contents entry for the Animals in Winter pages.

2. Cut out the title and glue it to the top of the page.

3. Cut out the *Remember* piece and glue it to the page below the title for reference.

4. Cut out the pockets. Apply glue to the backs of the three tabs and attach the pockets to the page. It may be helpful to fold on the dashed lines to create visual borders before applying the glue.

5. Cut out the picture cards. Look at the pictures on the pockets. Decide whether the animals on the cards hibernate (*Who is in the cave?, Who is in the tree?, Who is underground?*), migrate (*Who is flying south?*), or adapt (*Whose fur must change?*). Sort them into the correct pockets. Write *migrate, hibernate,* or *adapt* beside each pocket to tell what each animal is doing.

Reflect on Learning

To complete the left-hand page, have students draw lines to divide the page into three sections. Label each section *How I Migrate, How I Hibernate, and How I Adapt.* Each student should draw how she migrates (travels from place to place), hibernates (sleeps), and adapts (changes in some way).

Answer Key
Who is in the Tree? bat; *Who is in the cave?* bear, bat is also acceptable; *Whose fur must change?* hare, fox; *Who is flying south?* butterflies, geese; *Who is underground?* snake

Animals in Winter

Who is in the cave?

Who is in the tree?

Whose fur must change?

Who is underground?

Who is flying south?

Remember . . .
migrate = to move
hibernate = to sleep
adapt = to change

Holidays Around the World

Introduction

Read a book or watch a video about December holidays around the world. Compare the holidays in the book and video with how students celebrate their December holidays. Then, discuss the definition of a symbol as an object, a picture, or an action that represents something. Discuss common symbols of the holidays such as a Christmas tree, a menorah, etc. and what they stand for.

Creating the Notebook Page

Guide students through the following steps to complete the right-hand page in their notebooks.

1. Add a Table of Contents entry for the Holidays Around the World pages.

2. Cut out the title and glue it to the top of the page.

3. Cut out the story piece and glue it to the page below the title.

4. Cut out the pockets. Apply glue to the backs of the three tabs and attach the pockets to the page. It may be helpful to fold on the dashed lines to create visual borders before applying the glue.

5. Read the story about holiday traditions in other countries.

6. Cut out the picture cards. Look at the holiday traditions on the picture cards and decide which country the tradition represents. Sort the cards into the pockets with the flag of that country.

Reflect on Learning

To complete the left-hand page, have students draw symbols that would describe the December holiday that they celebrate. Allow time for students to share their drawings and explain why they chose their symbols.

Holidays Around the World

It is Christmas in America! People put lights on a tree. They hang stockings. They cook a turkey. In France, people light a fire. They eat cake shaped like a log. Santa wears a long robe. Children in the Netherlands put out a shoe filled with hay and carrots. It is for Santa's horse. They wear a crown with candles. The cookies look like windmills. Mexico has a party. They have a piñata. They eat a round cake. They give out pretty flowers.

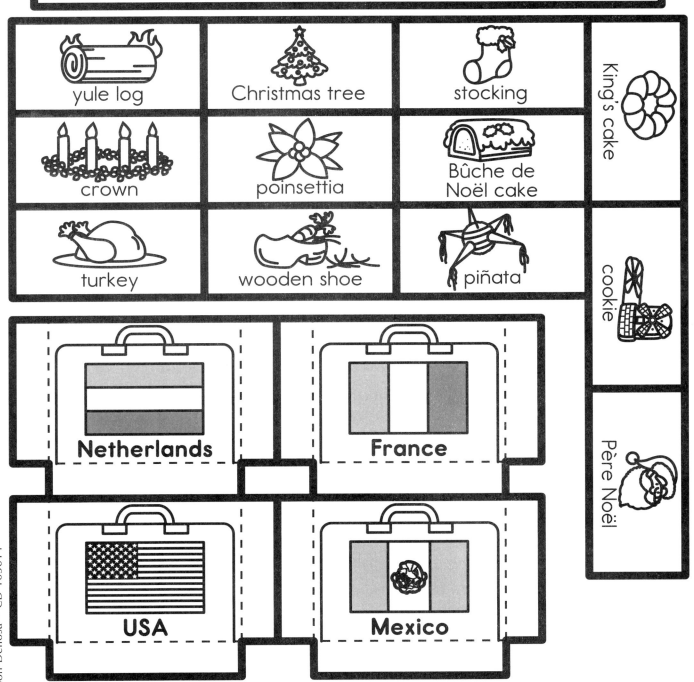

yule log

Christmas tree

stocking

King's cake

crown

poinsettia

Bûche de Noël cake

turkey

wooden shoe

piñata

cookie

Père Noël

Netherlands

France

USA

Mexico

Holiday Wants and Needs

Introduction

Have students describe to a partner a time they went shopping with a parent or guardian and asked for an item. Have students describe how they felt about the item. Then, discuss as a class what some of the items were and if they were things students wanted or needed. Review the difference between a want and a need. Because it can be a tricky concept, be sure to address food items like candy and chips that students may want but do not necessarily need, even though they are food.

Creating the Notebook Page

Guide students through the following steps to complete the right-hand page in their notebooks.

1. Add a Table of Contents entry for the Holiday Wants and Needs pages.

2. Cut out the title and glue it to the top of the page.

3. Cut out the *Needs/Wants* accordion fold. Fold back and forth on the dashed lines so each end panel meets in the center. The gift should show on top. Apply glue to the back of the center section and attach it to the page below the title.

4. Open the accordion fold. Read the definitions of *want* and *need*. In the center section beside the matching definition, draw an item you want and an item you need.

5. Cut out the *Wants* and *Needs* pockets. Apply glue to the backs of the three tabs and attach them to the page below the accordion fold. It may be helpful to fold on the dashed lines to create visual borders before applying the glue.

6. Cut out the gift tag pieces. Decide if each item is a want or a need and sort it into the correct pocket.

7. On the bottom of the page, write a sentence describing something you need. Then, write a sentence about something you want.

Reflect on Learning

To complete the left-hand page, gather holiday toy catalogs and store ads. Have students cut out one or more items they want and one or more items they need and glue them into their notebooks. Then, students should label each item *want* or *need* and describe why each is a want or need.

Wants and Needs

Things we would like to have, but can live without

Wants

Things we need to live and survive

Needs

Wants

Needs

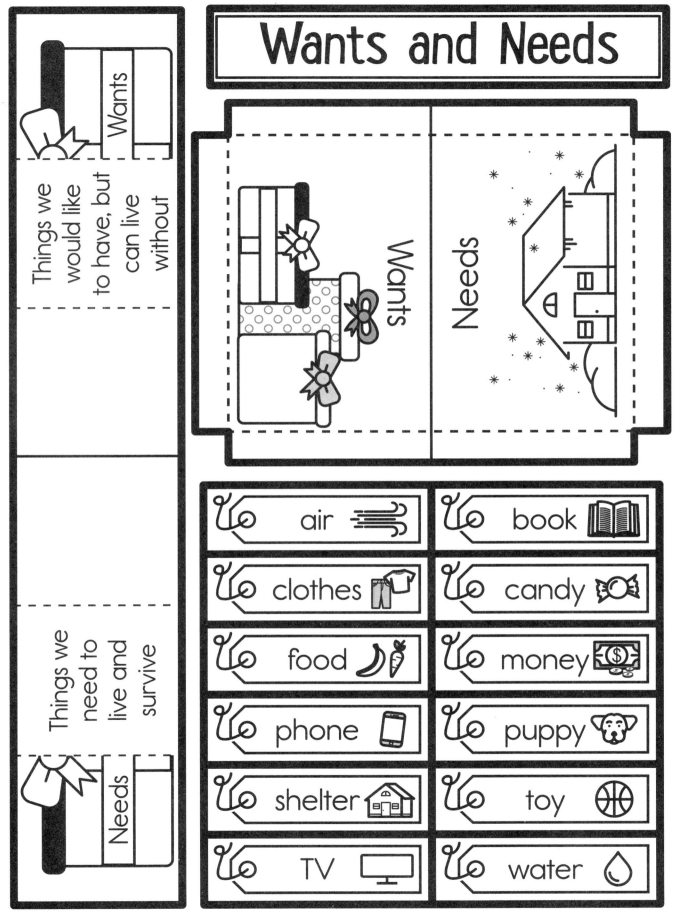

air

clothes

food

phone

shelter

TV

book

candy

money

puppy

toy

water

The Gingerbread Man: Story Elements

Introduction

Read the story of *The Gingerbread Man* together as a class. Create a giant gingerbread man on bulletin board paper and cut it into four large puzzle pieces. Write *Characters, Setting, Problem,* and *Solution* on each one of the four puzzle pieces. Divide the class into four groups. Give each group a piece of the puzzle. Each group should draw or write on the puzzle piece about their assigned story element. Have the groups put the puzzle together and discuss each one of the story elements.

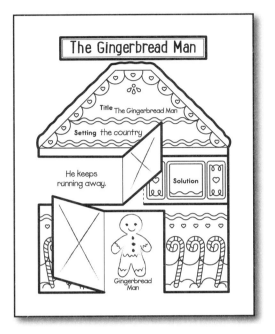

Creating the Notebook Page

Guide students through the following steps to complete the right-hand page in their notebooks.

1. Add a Table of Contents entry for The Gingerbread Man: Story Elements pages.

2. Cut out the title and glue it to the top of the page.

3. Cut out the gingerbread house piece. Cut on the solid lines to create the *Problem, Solution,* and *Main Character* flaps. On the backs of the flaps, draw an X. Apply glue to the back of each section of the gingerbread house that is not marked with an X and attach it to the page.

4. After reading or listening to *The Gingerbread Man,* write the title and setting on the top section of the house.

5. Name and draw the main character under the *Main Character* flap.

6. Write or draw the problem in the story under the *Problem* flap. Write or draw how the problem was resolved under the *Solution* flap.

Reflect on Learning

To complete the left-hand page, have students write or draw about another problem that could occur in *The Gingerbread Man*. Then, each student should write or draw a solution to his problem.

The Gingerbread Man

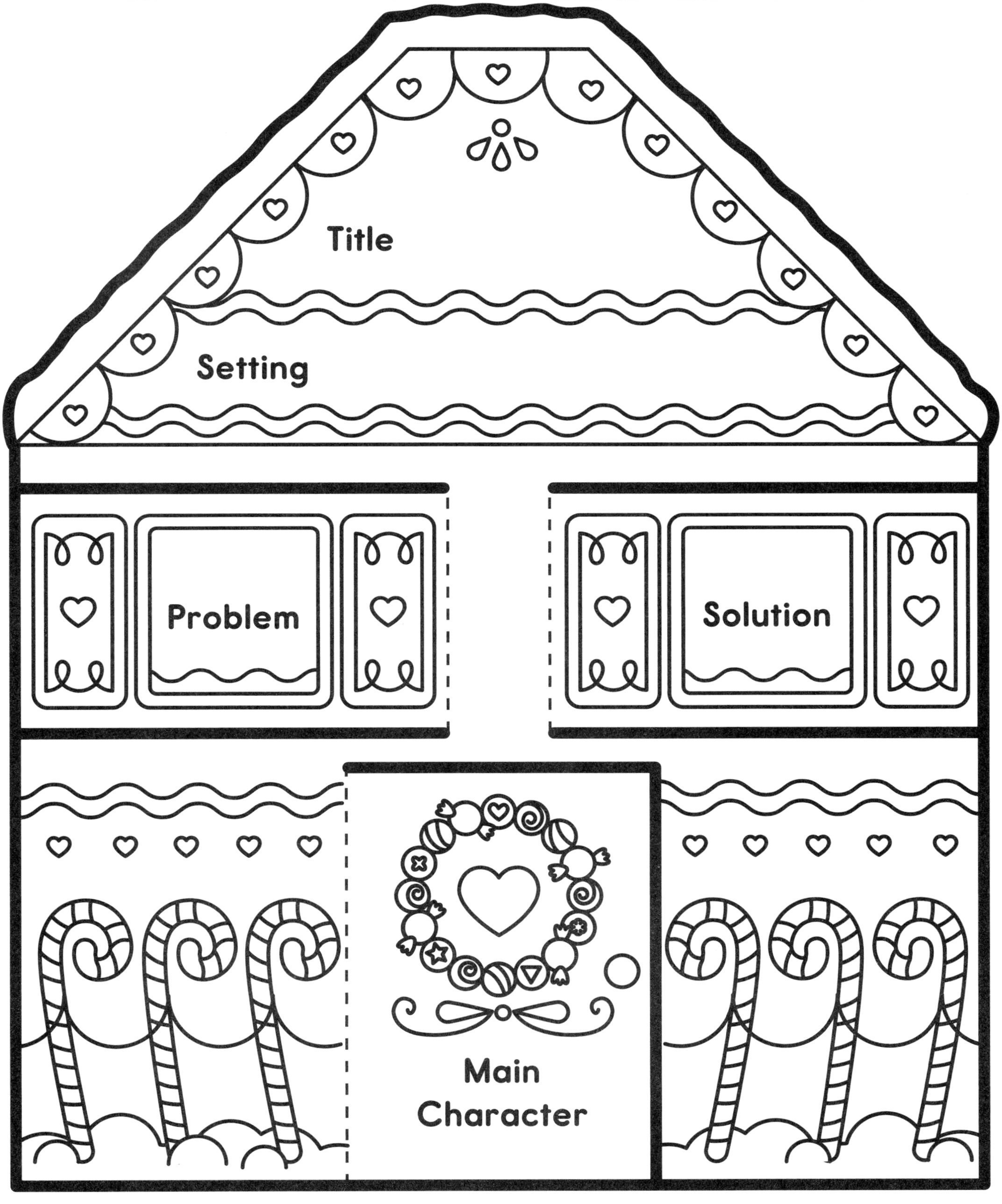

Title

Setting

Problem

Solution

Main Character

Verb Tense Snowmen

Introduction

Review the meaning of a verb (an action word). Explain that when the suffix *-ed* is added to a base word (the verb) it changes it to a verb that was done in the past. When the base word is used by itself it is a verb that is happening now. When *will* is added before the verb, the verb will happen in the future. Draw three circles on the board labeled *-ed, base word,* and *will.* Write various verbs on several sticky notes. Distribute them to a few students. Read a sentence using one of the verbs on the sticky notes such as *I am marching in place.* The student with the sticky note that says *march* should add *-ing* to the word and place his sticky note in the correct circle. If the sentence uses a base word in the present tense, then students should write nothing and place their words in the base word circle. Repeat the activity with the remaining verbs in various tenses.

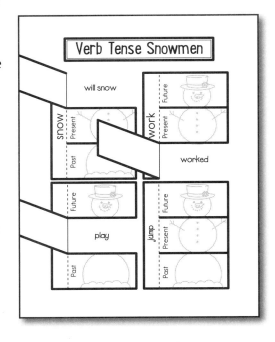

Creating the Notebook Page

Guide students through the following steps to complete the right-hand page in their notebooks.

1. Add a Table of Contents entry for the Verb Tense Snowmen pages.

2. Cut out the title and glue it to the top of the page.

3. Cut out the snowman flap books. Cut on the solid lines to create three flaps on each flap book. Apply glue to the backs of the narrow left sections and attach them to the page.

4. Read the verbs on the left side of each flap book. Under the *Past* flap, write the past tense of the word. Under the *Present* flap, write the present tense of the verb. Under the *Future* flap, write the future tense of the verb.

5. On the blank flap book, write another verb on the left side. Write the past, present, and future tenses under each flap.

Reflect on Learning

To complete the left-hand page, have students divide their page into three sections labeled *Past, Present,* and *Future.* Then, read three sentences with the verb *talk* used in each of the three tenses. For example, *I will talk to you later. I talked to him yesterday. You may talk to me now.* Students should record the correct tense in the appropriate section. Repeat the activity with two more verbs and sentence sets.

Verb Tense Snowmen

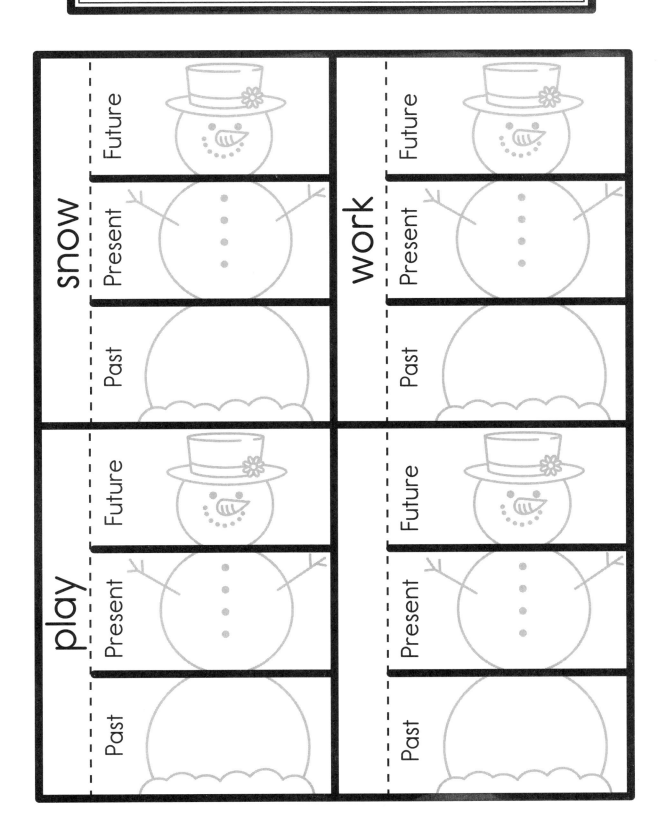

snow — Future — Present — Past

work — Future — Present — Past

play — Future — Present — Past

Future — Present — Past

Hot Chocolate Word Families

Caution: Before beginning any food activity, ask families' permission and inquire about students' food allergies and religious or other food restrictions.

Introduction

Review word families as words that have the same ending letters and sounds. Then, use sticky notes to program four large cups or mugs with four different word families. Distribute several mini-marshmallows to each student. Students should form a single line in front of the cups and toss a marshmallow towards the cups. Each time the marshmallow lands in a cup, the student should say a word in the corresponding word family.

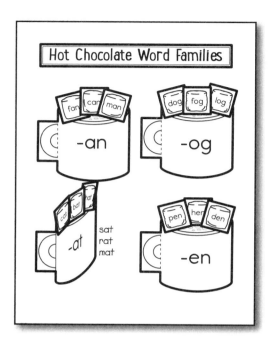

Creating the Notebook Page

Guide students through the following steps to complete the right-hand page in their notebooks.

1. Add a Table of Contents entry for the Hot Chocolate Word Families pages.

2. Cut out the title and glue it to the top of the page.

3. Cut out the mug pieces. Apply glue to the backs of the handle sections and attach them to the page.

4. Cut out the marshmallow pieces.

5. Read the words on the marshmallow pieces and say them out loud. Glue them to the top of each mug piece with the same word family.

6. Under the flaps, write other words that belong to each word family.

Reflect on Learning

To complete the left-hand page, write a word family such as *-ig* on the board. Have students write as many words as they can in 30 seconds that correspond with the word family. Repeat the activity with other word families.

Hot Chocolate Word Families

-an

-og

-at

-en

| dog | hen | fan | log | den | hat |
| can | cat | fog | bat | man | pen |

© Carson-Dellosa • CD-105014

Meet Phil and His Shadow

Introduction

Explain that shadows form when light from the sun is blocked by an object. Turn off the lights, leaving on a projector or a flashlight. Tell students to pretend the light is the sun and show them how to make shadow puppets with their hands. Emphasize how their hands block the light, which creates shadows in the shapes of their hands.

Creating the Notebook Page

Guide students through the following steps to complete the right-hand page in their notebooks.

1. Add a Table of Contents entry for the Meet Phil and His Shadow pages.

2. Cut out the title and glue it to the top of the page.

3. Cut out the story piece. Glue it to the page below the title.

4. Cut out the pockets. Apply glue to the backs of the three tabs and attach the pockets to the page. It may be helpful to fold on the dashed lines to create visual borders before applying the glue.

5. Cut out the groundhog pieces. Sort each groundhog piece into the pocket showing its matching shadow.

Reflect on Learning

To complete the left-hand page, have students write or draw what Phil's shadow would look like at different times of the day and why.

Meet Phil and His Shadow

Phil is a special groundhog. On Groundhog Day, people want to know if Phil will see his shadow. If he sees his shadow, that means six more weeks of winter. Brr! If he does not see his shadow, that means spring is coming!

Counting 100 Seconds of Fun

Introduction

Distribute various small items such as o-shaped cereal, paper clips, coin manipulatives, etc. at two or three different stations in the room. Allow students to rotate through the stations with partners. Have pairs of students practice counting to 100 by counting out 100 of the object at each station.

Creating the Notebook Page

Guide students through the following steps to complete the right-hand page in their notebooks.

1. Add a Table of Contents entry for the Counting 100 Seconds of Fun pages.

2. Cut out the title and glue it to the top of the page.

3. Cut out the *In 100 seconds, I can . . .* flap book. Cut on the solid lines to create three flaps on each side. Apply glue to the back of the center section and attach it to the page below the title.

4. Cut out the hundred chart. Glue it to the page below the flap book.

5. Read the task on each flap. Have a friend count aloud to 100 using the hundred chart. Under the flap, write how many times you completed the task in the given time. Use a separate sheet of paper for the writing task. Repeat until all of the tasks are complete.

Reflect on Learning

To complete the left-hand page, give each student a blank (or partially filled) hundred chart to glue in their notebooks. Students should fill in the hundred chart with the correct numbers.

Counting 100 Seconds of Fun

clap my hands.	In 100 seconds, I can . . .	write my name.
count to 10.		sing the alphabet.
touch my toes.		jump up and down.

1	2	3	4	5	6	7	8	9	10
11	12	13	14	15	16	17	18	19	20
21	22	23	24	25	26	27	28	29	30
31	32	33	34	35	36	37	38	39	40
41	42	43	44	45	46	47	48	49	50
51	52	53	54	55	56	57	58	59	60
61	62	63	64	65	66	67	68	69	70
71	72	73	74	75	76	77	78	79	80
81	82	83	84	85	86	87	88	89	90
91	92	93	94	95	96	97	98	99	100

3/26/2020

Valentine's Day Doubles Facts

Introduction

Remind students that knowing their doubles facts can help them solve math problems more easily. Program six large sheets of construction paper with the numbers 1 through 6. Tape them in place on the floor in a row at the front of the room. Have students form a single line at the beginning of the row. Play a short piece of music as students walk on the row of numbers and back around to the back of the line. Periodically stop the music. When the music stops, the students who are standing on a number should give the doubles facts for the number they are standing on. Continue the activity a few more times.

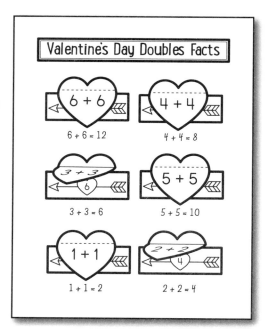

Creating the Notebook Page

Guide students through the following steps to complete the right-hand page in their notebooks.

1. Add a Table of Contents entry for the Valentine's Day Doubles Facts pages.

2. Cut out the title and glue it to the top of the page.

3. Cut out the heart flaps. Apply glue to the backs of the top sections and attach them to the page.

4. Cut out the arrow pieces.

5. Look at the doubles addition problem on each flap. Solve the problem and find the arrow with the matching sum. Glue each arrow sum under the flap with its doubles addition problem.

6. Rewrite each doubles fact on the page below the heart.

Reflect on Learning

To complete the left-hand page, have students draw or write to answer the following question: *How does knowing doubles facts help me know the answer to 4 + 5 = ?*

Valentine's Day Doubles Facts

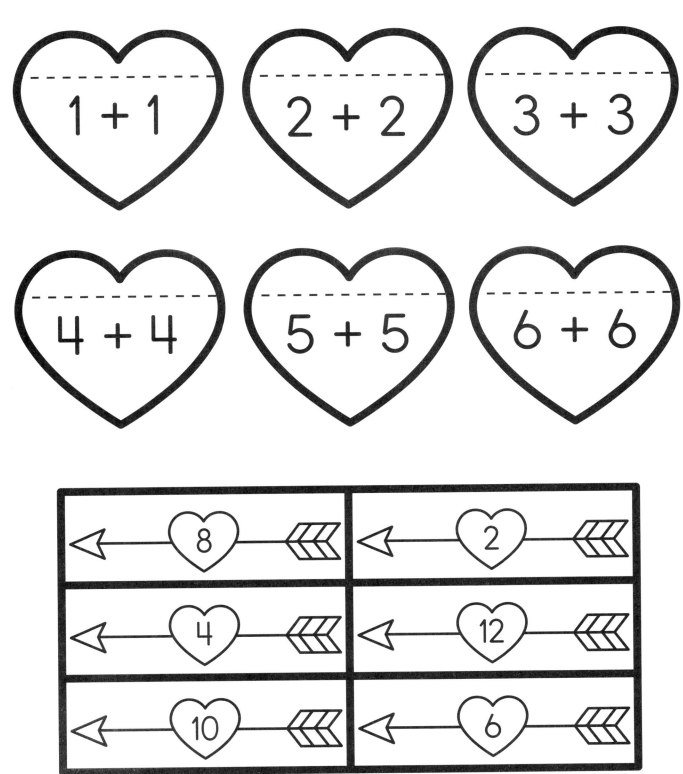

1 + 1

2 + 2

3 + 3

4 + 4

5 + 5

6 + 6

8

2

4

12

10

6

Presidents' Day

Introduction

Discuss the lives of George Washington and Abraham Lincoln. Draw a Venn diagram on the board. Write *George* on one side and *Abe* on the other side. As a class, compare and contrast the two presidents using what students already know about the two men. Discuss the similarities and differences after completing the diagram.

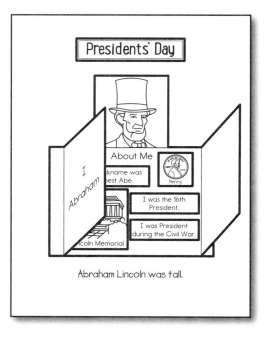

Creating the Notebook Page

Guide students through the following steps to complete the right-hand page in their notebooks.

1. Add a Table of Contents entry for the Presidents' Day pages.

2. Cut out the title and glue it to the top of the page.

3. Cut out the *About Me* pieces for each president book. Glue them to two different pages in your notebook.

4. Cut out the *I Am* flaps for each book. These will be the covers of the President books.

5. Apply glue to the gray glue sections of each *About Me* piece. Attach the *I Am* flaps to each President book, placing them side by side so that the inside edges of the pieces align.

6. Cut out the fact and picture cards for each president. Read the facts and look at the pictures. Decide whether they are about George Washington or Abraham Lincoln. Glue the cards into the correct *About Me* President books.

7. Write or draw another fact about each president below the President book.

Reflect on Learning

To complete the left-hand page, ask students to choose either Lincoln or Washington and write or draw to explain why he is their favorite of the two presidents.

Presidents' Day

About Me

My nickname was Honest Abe.

I was the 16th President.

I was President during the Civil War.

Lincoln Memorial

Penny

glue

glue

About Me

I was the first President.

I was a founding father.

I helped win the Revolutionary War.

Washington Monument

Quarter

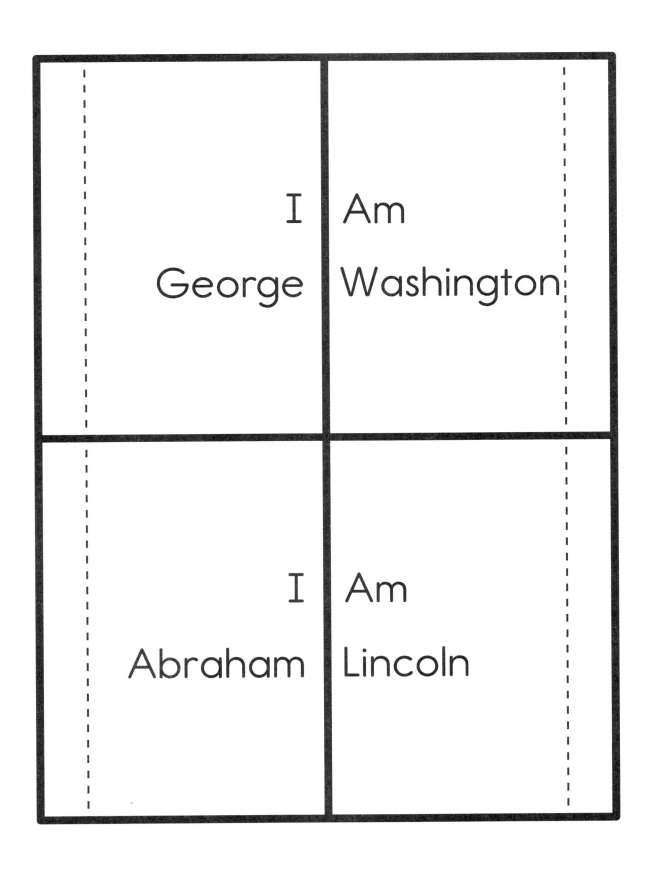

I Am
George Washington

I Am
Abraham Lincoln

Jackie Robinson Vowel Teams

Introduction

Write the words *keep* and *leaf* on the board. Ask students what they notice about the two words. Explain that the long *e* sound can be made by combining two vowel sounds. This is called a vowel team because the two vowels work together to make a new long vowel sound. Program two pieces of construction paper with an *e* and an *a*. Two student volunteers should come to the front of the room. Have one student hold an *e* and the other student hold an *a*. Say the word *team*. The two students should walk together (with the student holding the *e* on the left) around the room as you remind students that when two vowels go walking, the first one does the talking.

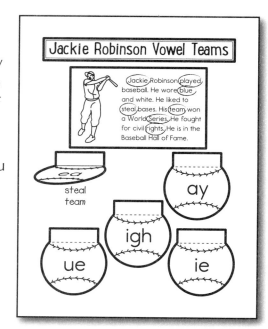

Creating the Notebook Page

Guide students through the following steps to complete the right-hand page in their notebooks.

1. Add a Table of Contents entry for the Jackie Robinson Vowel Teams pages.

2. Cut out the title and glue it to the top of the page.

3. Cut out the story piece. Glue it to the page below the title.

4. Cut out the baseball flaps. Apply glue to the backs of the top sections and attach them to the page.

5. Look at the vowel team on each baseball flap. Read the story about Jackie Robinson and circle words that contain the vowel teams on the baseball flaps. Write the circled words under the correct flaps. (Note: The *ea* and *ie* flaps will contain two words.)

Reflect on Learning

To complete the left-hand page, have students draw five big circles (baseballs). Label the circles *ie*, *ay*, *ea*, *igh*, and *ue*. Say the following words and have students write or draw the word in the correct circle: *hay, pie, leaf, glue, light*.

Answer Key
ie–Jackie, Series; ay–played; ea–steal, team; igh–rights; ue–blue

Jackie Robinson Vowel Teams

Jackie Robinson played baseball. He wore blue and white. He liked to steal bases. His team won a World Series. He fought for civil rights. He is in the Baseball Hall of Fame.

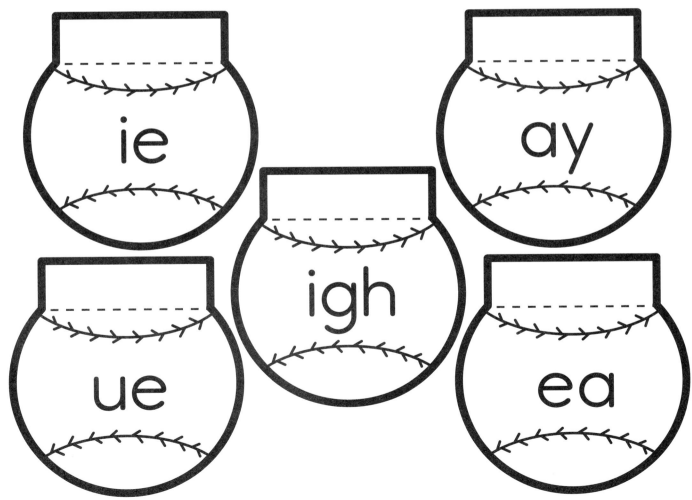

ie

ay

igh

ue

ea

Hatching Prefixes and Suffixes

Introduction

Review prefixes and suffixes. Have students act out words with prefixes and suffixes. For example, write the word *happy* on the board. Then, write *un* in front of the word *happy*. Students should act out each word and discuss the new meaning. Then, give students a blank sheet of paper. Tell students that their papers are *colorless*. Then, have them color the paper with several different colors. Now, tell students that their papers are *colorful*.

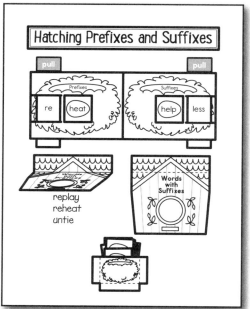

Creating the Notebook Page

Guide students through the following steps to complete the right-hand page in their notebooks.

1. Add a Table of Contents entry for the Hatching Prefixes and Suffixes pages.

2. Cut out the title and glue it to the top of the page.

3. Cut out the two nest pieces. Cut on the solid lines to create the slits for the pull strips. Apply glue to the backs of the larger left or right sections and the center flap on the left or right side. Attach the *Prefixes* piece to the left-hand side of the page below the title. Attach the *Suffixes* piece beside the *Prefixes* nest piece. The top and bottom flaps on the left or right side should open freely.

4. Cut out the two *pull* strips. Insert the correct *pull* strip into the slits so that only one prefix or suffix shows at a time.

5. Cut out the two birdhouses. Apply glue to the backs of the top sections and attach them to the page below the two nests.

6. Cut out the nest pocket. Apply glue to the backs of the three tabs and attach it to the page below the birdhouses. It may be helpful to fold on the dashed lines to create visual borders before applying the glue.

7. Cut out the egg cards. Place them in the nest pocket.

8. For each prefix and suffix nest, pull a word card from the pocket. Place it on the nest in the gray area. Pull the strip up or down to make words with the prefix or suffix. If the prefix or suffix makes a real word, write it under the correct birdhouse flap.

9. Store the word cards and the pull strips in the nest pocket when not in use.

Reflect on Learning

To complete the left-hand page, write the following words on the board: *kind, unkind, helpless,* and *helpful*. Have students illustrate the meaning of each word and label each drawing with the word.

Hatching Prefixes and Suffixes

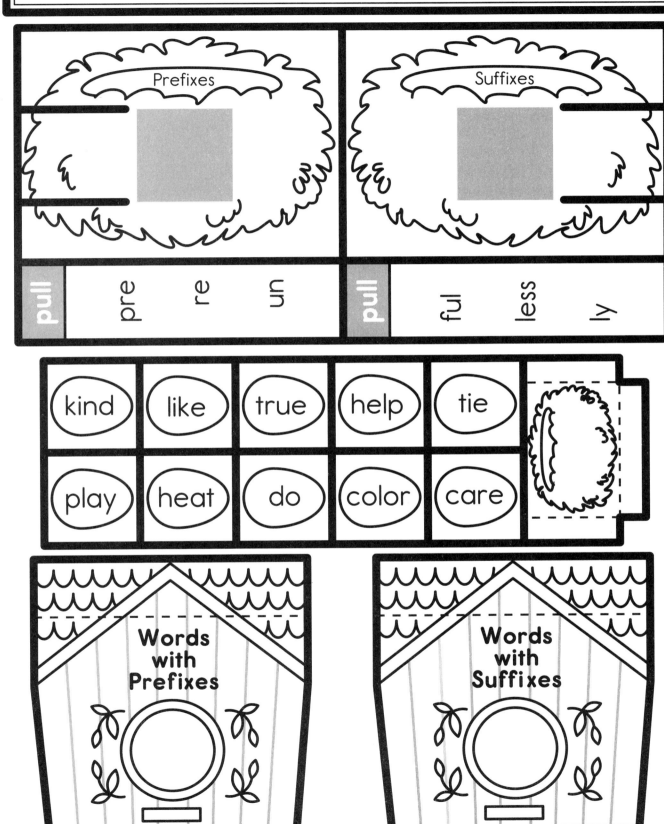

Prefixes

Suffixes

pull

pre   re   un

pull

ful   less   ly

kind   like   true   help   tie

play   heat   do   color   care

Words with Prefixes

Words with Suffixes

Lucky Blends and Digraphs

Introduction

Review blends as two letters that blend together. Both of the sounds can be heard. Review digraphs as two letters together that make one new sound. Say the word *blend*. Write it on the board and circle the *nd*. Say the word *digraph*. Write it on the board and circle the *ph*. Remind students that this is an easy way to remember the two because they both end in a blend or a digraph. Then, show pictures of objects with names that have blends and digraphs in them, such as grapes or a peach. Have students tell you whether the sound heard in the name is a blend or a digraph. Remind students that blends and digraphs can occur anywhere in a word.

Creating the Notebook Page

Guide students through the following steps to complete the right-hand page in their notebooks.

1. Add a Table of Contents entry for the Lucky Blends and Digraphs pages.

2. Cut out the title and glue it to the top of the page.

3. Cut out the *Is it a Blend? OR Is it a Digraph?* flap book. Apply glue to the back of the center section and attach it to the page below the title.

4. Cut out the definition cards. Decide whether the card defines a blend or a digraph. Glue them under the matching flaps.

5. Cut out the word cards. Read the words and decide whether the word contains a blend or a digraph. Glue them to the page in columns below the blend and digraph flaps. Underline the blend or digraph.

6. Use the blank pot of gold pieces to write more words containing blends and digraphs, glue them into the correct columns, and underline the blend or digraph.

Reflect on Learning

To complete the left-hand page, have students draw lines to divide their pages in half. Label the sides *blends* and *digraphs*. Write several words with blends and digraphs on the board such as *flower, clap, tooth,* and *sheep*. Have students write the words into the correct columns and circle the blends or digraphs. If desired, students can illustrate each word.

Lucky Blends and Digraphs

Is it a blend? **OR** Is it a digraph?

| Two letters together that make one new sound | Two letters that blend together and both sounds can be heard. |

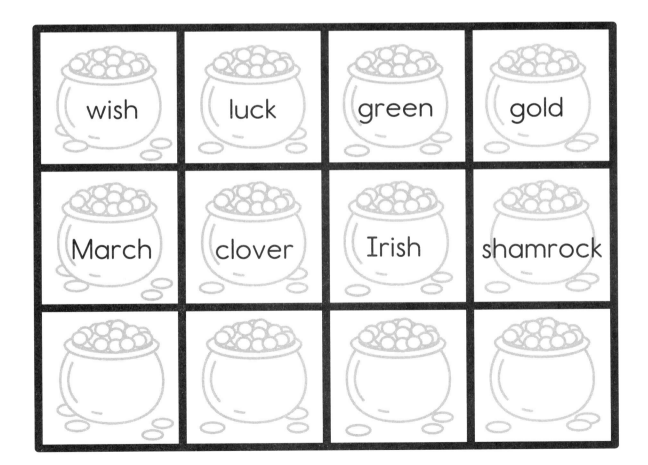

wish | luck | green | gold

March | clover | Irish | shamrock

Spring Weather Is in the Air

Introduction

Draw a cloud on the board. Write *Weather Types* in the middle of the cloud. Have students tell you the different types of weather (rainy, cloudy, foggy, windy, sunny, and snowy). Record their answers in clouds on the board under the *Weather Types* cloud. Discuss how weather is measured by specific weather tools such as a thermometer, rain gauge, or weather vane. Then, divide the class into six groups. Assign each group a weather type. Each group should create a poster to describe the type of weather they were given. The posters should include what the weather type looks like and what activities might be taking place during that type of weather. Have groups share their posters with the class.

Creating the Notebook Page

Guide students through the following steps to complete the right-hand page in their notebooks.

1. Add a Table of Contents entry for the Spring Weather Is in the Air pages.

2. Cut out the title and glue it to the top of the page.

3. Cut out the flap book. Cut on the solid lines to create four flaps on each side. Place the piece face down. Fold the flaps in so they align in the center. Apply glue to the gray glue section on the back and attach it to the page.

4. Read the weather type on the left side. Then, draw it on the right side.

5. Cut out the four larger description cards. Decide which type of weather each card describes. Glue them inside the flap book under the matching flaps.

6. Cut out the *Measuring Weather* flap book. Cut on the solid lines to create three flaps. Apply glue to the back of the top section and attach it to the page.

7. Cut out the three smaller description cards. Look at the weather tools on each flap on the *Measuring Weather* flap book. Match each description with its tool and glue it under the flap.

Reflect on Learning

To complete the left-hand page, have students draw a picture to illustrate their favorite type of weather. Students should explain the type of weather it is and why it is their favorite. Have students also draw the weather tool(s) used to measure their favorite weather.

Spring Is in the Air

sunny

windy

cloudy

rainy

glue

The clouds are low and gray. Rain is falling from the sky.

The clouds are blocking the sun. The air may be cooler.

The air is warm. The sun is shining brightly in the sky.

Trees are swaying. Objects may be moving through the air.

Measuring Weather

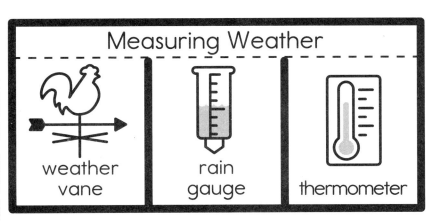

weather vane

rain gauge

thermometer

measures the temperature

measures how much rain is falling

shows which way the wind is moving

Butterfly 10 More, 10 Less

Introduction

Show a hundred chart. Model how to find 10 more and 10 less from a base number. Then, program index cards with numbers so there are three cards in each set: the base number, 10 more, and 10 less. For example, one set of cards might be numbered *34*, *44*, and *54*. Give each student one card. Have students walk around and find the other two students with the corresponding numbers to complete their set.

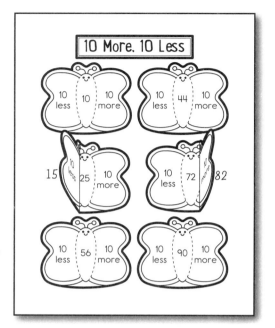

Creating the Notebook Page

Guide students through the following steps to complete the right-hand page in their notebooks.

1. Add a Table of Contents entry for the Butterfly 10 More, 10 Less pages.

2. Cut out the title and glue it to the top of the page.

3. Cut out the butterfly pieces. Apply glue to the backs of the center sections and attach them to the page.

4. Look at the number on each butterfly. Under the *10 less* flap, write the number that is 10 less than that number. Under the *10 more* flap, write the number that is 10 more than that number.

Reflect on Learning

To complete the left-hand page, have students draw lines to divide their page into three columns. Give each student two number cubes or dice. Students should roll the dice or number cubes and record the two-digit number in the middle column. Then, have students record the number that is 10 less in the first column and 10 more in the last column. Encourage students to use a hundred chart as a resource if needed. Repeat the activity several times for additional practice.

10 More, 10 Less

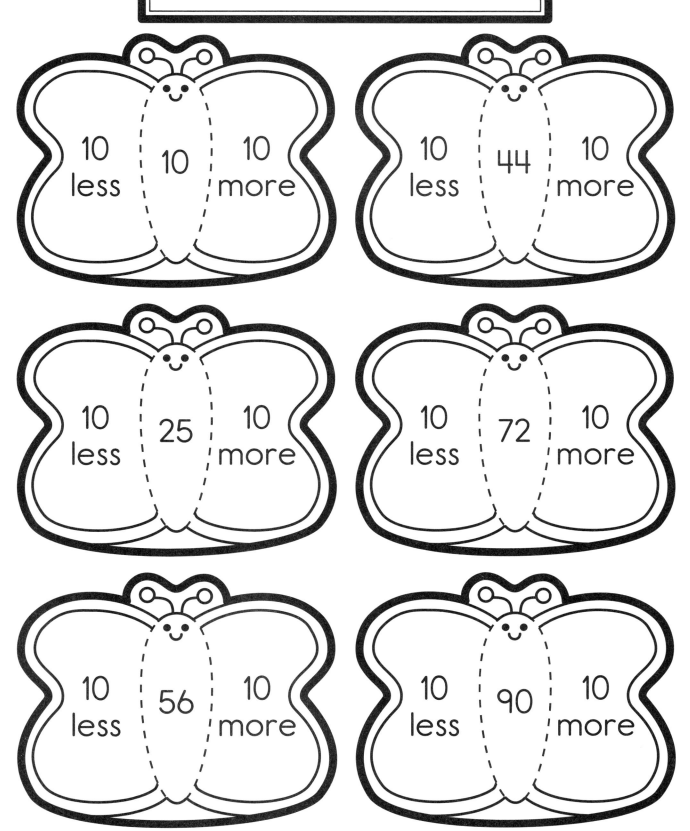

10 less	10	10 more
10 less	44	10 more
10 less	25	10 more
10 less	72	10 more
10 less	56	10 more
10 less	90	10 more

Spring Magic: Butterfly Life Cycle

Introduction

Review the four stages of the butterfly life cycle. Then, distribute a paper plate to each student. Students should draw lines to divide the paper plate into four equal sections. Starting in the first left-hand section, have students draw and color a leaf. Then, glue a small round pasta shell (ditalini pasta) onto the leaf in the first section. Label the section *egg*. Continuing clockwise, students should continue to draw a leaf, glue pasta, and label the stages in the next two sections. (Use corkscrew pasta for *caterpillar* and shell pasta for *chrysalis*.) Finally, have students glue a butterfly-shaped pasta (farfalle or bow-tie pasta) into the last section and label it *butterfly*.

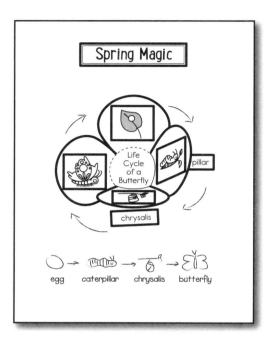

Creating the Notebook Page

Guide students through the following steps to complete the right-hand page in their notebooks.

1. Add a Table of Contents entry for the Spring Magic: Butterfly Life Cycle pages.

2. Cut out the title and glue it to the top of the page.

3. Cut out the *Life Cycle of a Butterfly* piece on the solid lines. Apply glue to the back of the center section and attach it to the page.

4. Cut out the word and picture cards.

5. Glue the picture cards on the flaps in the order of a butterfly's life cycle.

6. Glue the word cards under the flaps that show the matching life cycle stage.

7. Draw arrows in between the flaps to show the direction of the stages in the butterfly life cycle.

Reflect on Learning

To complete the left-hand page, have students write or draw to answer the following question: *Do you think the butterfly life cycle ever ends? Why or why not?*

Spring Magic

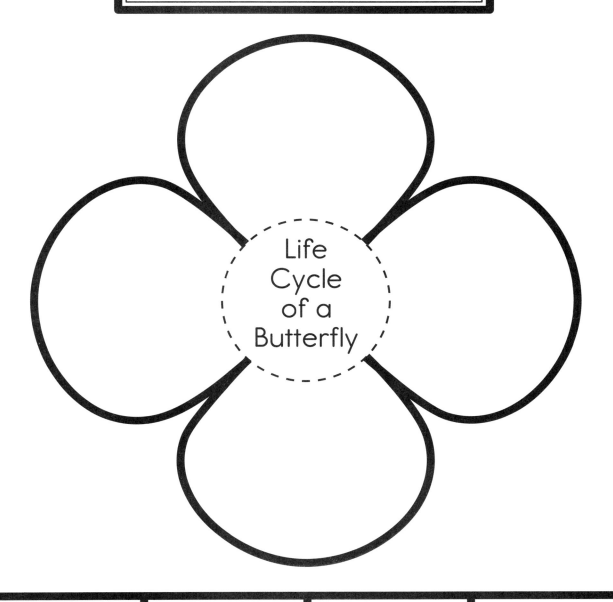

Life Cycle of a Butterfly

| butterfly | caterpillar | chrysalis | egg |

Rainy Day Place Value

Introduction

Review the values of the ones cubes and the tens rods from base ten blocks. Then, distribute several ones cubes and tens rods to each student. Tell students the following story and have them act out each part with tens rods and ones cubes as you read. (It may be helpful to write each number on the board as it is introduced.) *Sara had a pool party in her backyard with 12 friends. Her mother made 24 cupcakes for the party. Just as Sara and her friends were about to throw 30 dive sticks into the pool, it started to thunder. All 13 of them made it back into the house before it began to pour down rain!*

Creating the Notebook Page

Guide students through the following steps to complete the right-hand page in their notebooks.

1.   Add a Table of Contents entry for the Rainy Day Place Value pages.

2.   Cut out the title and glue it to the top of the page.

3.   Cut out the cloud flaps. Apply glue to the backs of the top sections and attach them to the page. Leave enough space for the raindrops to fit on the page below each flap.

4.   Cut out the tens and ones raindrop pieces.

5.   Look at the number on each cloud. Find the tens and ones that compose the number. Glue them below the cloud.

6.   Write the tens and ones addition sentence that represents each number under each flap.

Reflect on Learning

To complete the left-hand page, have each student draw a cloud and write *42* in it. Students should draw tens rods and ones cubes to represent the number. Then, have students write the corresponding number sentence.

Rainy Day Place Value

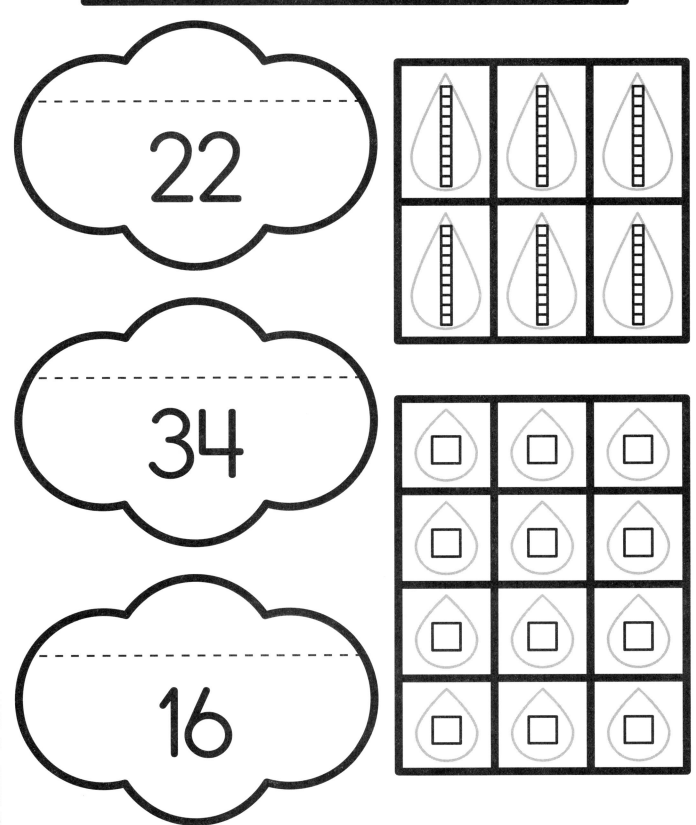

22

34

16

Going Green

Introduction

Discuss how Earth stays cleaner and greener when garbage is disposed of the right way. Review what it means to recycle. Then, discuss the concept of composting. Explain that materials such as leaves, fruits and vegetable scraps, flowers, grass cuttings, and egg shells can be put into a composting pile. These materials break down and create a rich soil. People can then use the soil around their flowers, in gardens, etc. Remind students that some things cannot break down, such as glass, metal, plastics, and meat scraps. Then, distribute pictures of various items such as egg shells, used batteries, plastic soda cans, etc. to students. Provide three baskets marked as *Recycle, Trash*, and *Composting*. Have students take turns putting their pictures into the correct baskets.

Creating the Notebook Page

Guide students through the following steps to complete the right-hand page in their notebooks.

1. Add a Table of Contents entry for the Going Green pages.

2. Cut out the title and glue it to the top of the page.

3. Cut out the definitions piece. Glue it to the page below the title to use as a reference.

4. Cut out the *Trash, Recycle, Compost* flap book. Cut on the solid lines to create three flaps. Apply glue to the back of the left side and attach it to the page.

5. Cut out the picture cards. Sort which objects are best for trash, recycling, or composting. Glue them under the corresponding flaps.

6. Cut out the globe flap book. Cut on the solid line to create two flaps. Apply glue to the back of the top section and attach it to the bottom of the page.

7. Under the happy globe flap, write or draw things that are good for the planet. Under the sad globe flap, write or draw things that are bad for the planet.

Reflect on Learning

To complete the left-hand page, have students draw posters to show ways they can help Earth by going green.

Answer Key
Trash: potato chip bag, broken plate, adhesive bandage; Recycle: can, plastic bag, cereal box; Compost: banana peel, apple core, grass and leaves

Going Green

trash: food or other items that are thrown away and not reused

recycle: to make something new from something used

compost: a mixture of leaves, grass, and discarded food that helps to improve garden soil

Trash

Recycle

Compost

Shades of Meaning

Introduction

Review how some words can mean almost the same thing. Then, have students act out the following emotions: happy, cheerful, joyful, and merry. Discuss what was the same and different about how the emotions were acted out. Repeat the activity again with students acting out the actions of walking, marching, hiking, and strolling.

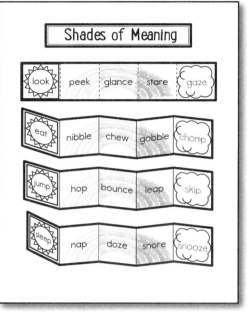

Creating the Notebook Page

Guide students through the following steps to complete the right-hand page in their notebooks.

1. Add a Table of Contents entry for the Shades of Meaning pages.

2. Cut out the title and glue it to the top of the page.

3. Cut out the rainbow accordion folds. Fold on the dashed lines, alternating the fold direction so that the blank panel is on the front. Apply glue to the back of the last section and attach it to the page.

4. Cut out the sun word cards. Read the words and match them with their shades of meaning rainbow accordion folds. Glue them to the blank end of each rainbow.

5. Color the rainbows. As the meanings of the words get stronger, color the rainbow darker. Start with a colored pencil for the first word, use a crayon for the second word, and use a marker for the last word.

6. Write another word in the cloud at the end of each rainbow that means almost the same thing as the other words in each rainbow.

Reflect on Learning

To complete the left-hand page, have students draw pictures to illustrate the following adjectives: *scared, afraid, frightened,* and *terrified.* Have students label their pictures with the adjectives.

Shades of Meaning

jump   eat   sleep   look

snore   leap   gobble   stare

doze   bounce   chew   glance

nap   hop   nibble   peek

Sun Power: Nonfiction

Introduction

Discuss the different elements between fiction and nonfiction. Show students a few books from both genres and have students tell you whether the book is fiction or nonfiction. Discuss the definitions of *topic, main idea, key detail, genre,* and *author's purpose*. Create an anchor chart together as a class titled *Elements of Nonfiction* as you discuss the definitions.

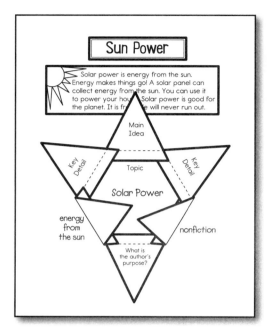

Creating the Notebook Page

Guide students through the following steps to complete the right-hand page in their notebooks.

1. Add a Table of Contents entry for the Sun Power: Nonfiction pages.

2. Cut out the title and glue it to the top of the page.

3. Cut out the passage piece. Glue it to the page below the title.

4. Cut out the *Topic* piece. Glue it to the page, leaving room for the flaps to be placed around it.

5. Cut out the flaps. Apply glue to the backs of the narrow sections and attach them around the *Topic* piece to create a sun-shaped flap book.

6. Read the passage about sun power. Write the topic in the center of the flap book. Under each flap, write the corresponding story element from the passage or answer the question on the flap.

Reflect on Learning

To complete the left-hand page, have students read the passage on the right-hand page again. Then, students should draw a picture to illustrate the main points of the passage.

Sun Power

Solar power is energy from the sun. Energy makes things go! A solar panel can collect energy from the sun. You can use it to power your house. Solar power is good for the planet. It is free. We will never run out.

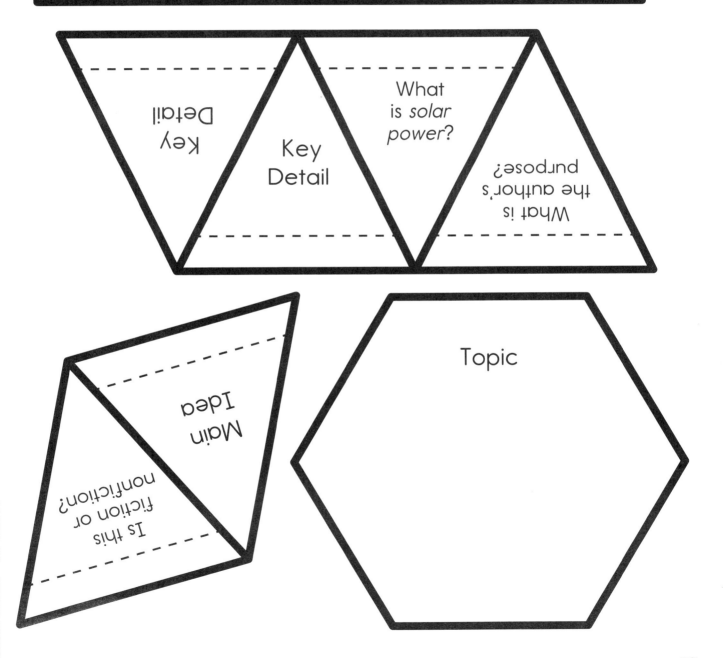

Key Detail

Key Detail

What is *solar power*?

What is the author's purpose?

Main Idea

Is this fiction or nonfiction?

Topic

Sporty Measurement

Introduction

Review measuring with nonstandard measurement units. Demonstrate how to line up the measuring unit end to end to get the correct measurement. Then, draw a few objects on the board both horizontally and vertically such as a worm, a pencil, etc. Give volunteers several sticky notes. Have them line up the sticky notes end to end to measure the various objects. Then, the students should count the sticky notes and record their measurements on the board under or beside each object.

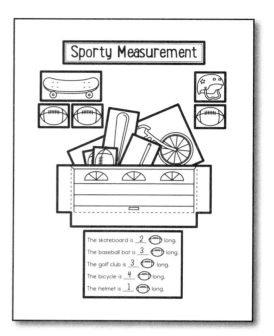

Creating the Notebook Page

Guide students through the following steps to complete the right-hand page in their notebooks.

1. Add a Table of Contents entry for the Sporty Measurement pages.

2. Cut out the title and glue it to the top of the page.

3. Cut out the garage pocket. Apply glue to the backs of the three tabs and attach the pocket to the page. It may be helpful to fold on the dashed lines to create visual borders before applying the glue.

4. Cut out *The skateboard is* piece and glue it to the page below the pocket.

5. Cut out the objects and football pieces. Measure the length of each object by lining up the football pieces side by side. Record the measurements on *The skateboard is* piece.

6. Store the picture cards and football pieces in the garage pocket when not in use.

Reflect on Learning

To complete the left-hand page, assign students several objects such as pencils, crayons, markers, etc. to measure. Students should use linking cubes to measure the objects. Then, have students draw the objects they measured in the notebooks and record the measurement.

Sporty Measurement

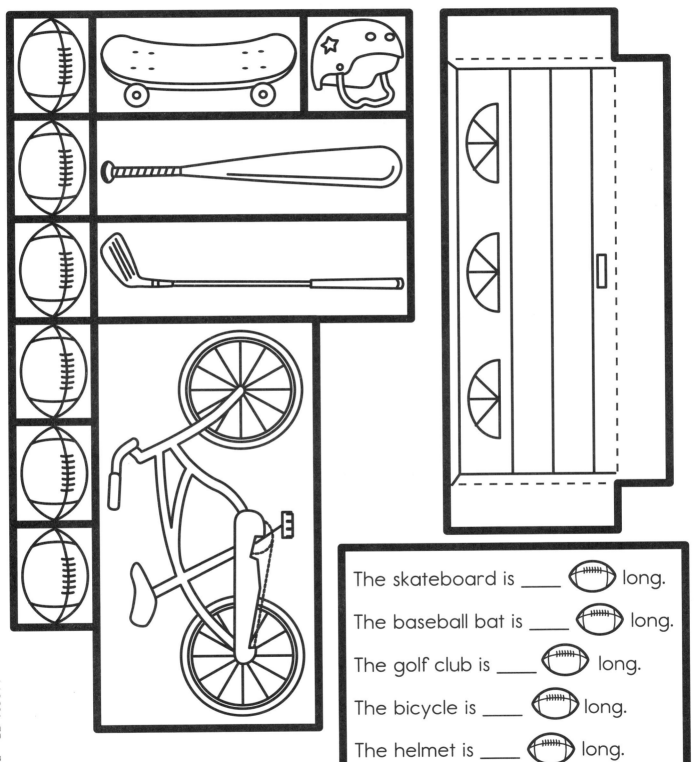

The skateboard is ____ 🏈 long.

The baseball bat is ____ 🏈 long.

The golf club is ____ 🏈 long.

The bicycle is ____ 🏈 long.

The helmet is ____ 🏈 long.

Beach Fun Shapes

Introduction

Draw a hexagon on the board. Model how to identify and count the attributes such as 6 sides, 6 angles, etc. Add labels. Then, draw a model of a sphere. Identify the attributes of the sphere, pointing out that the sphere has no sides, angles, vertices (corners), or faces. Then, assign student groups various shapes. Each group should make a poster to show the attributes of the assigned shape and draw real-world objects that look like the shape.

Creating the Notebook Page

Guide students through the following steps to complete the right-hand page in their notebooks.

1. Add a Table of Contents entry for the Beach Fun Shapes pages.

2. Cut out the title and glue it to the top of the page.

3. Cut out the pockets. Apply glue to the backs of the three tabs on each pocket and attach them to the page. It may be helpful to fold on the dashed lines to create visual borders before applying the glue. Leave space to place a picture card by each pocket.

4. Cut out the shape names. Sort them into the correct pockets.

5. Cut out the shape properties cards. Read the clues on the cards and then sort them into the correct pockets.

6. Cut out the picture cards. Glue them next to the shape pocket that matches the real-world object shown.

Reflect on Learning

To complete the left-hand page, assign each student a shape. Then, he should name and draw the shape and label the attributes. Finally, he should draw real-world objects that look like the shape.

Beach Fun Shapes

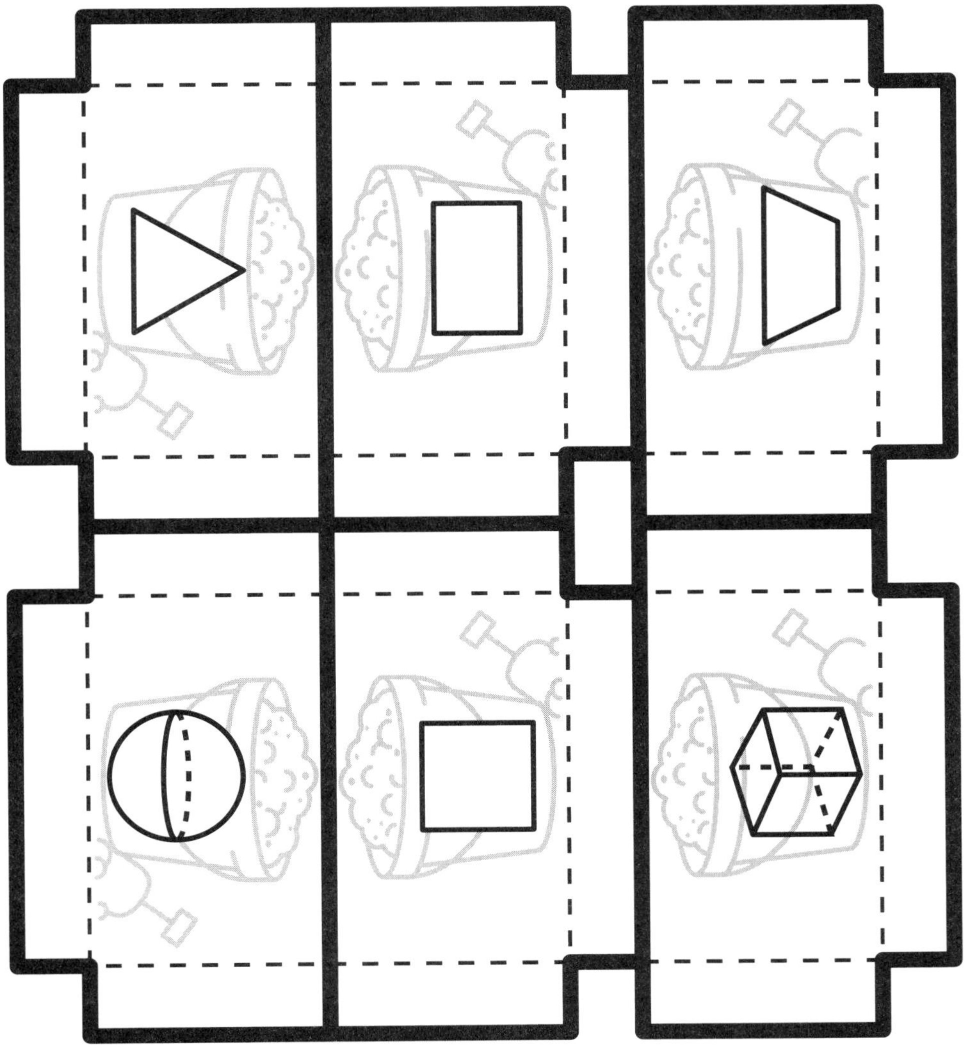

trapezoid

cube

sphere

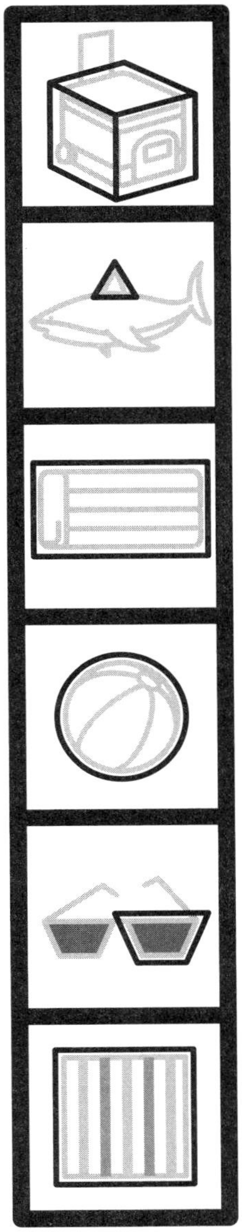

| rectangle | square | triangle |

2 equal sides, 2 unequal sides

4 equal sides

3 corners

solid shape, no angles

solid shape, 8 corners

4 corners, opposite sides are equal

Give Me Liberty: Comparing

Introduction

Discuss the words *liberty* and *freedom*. Give each student a blank sheet of paper. Have students write the following on the top of their paper: *Freedom means* _____ . Students should finish the sentence and then illustrate it. Allow time for students to share their drawings.

Creating the Notebook Page

Guide students through the following steps to complete the right-hand page in their notebooks.

1. Add a Table of Contents entry for the Give Me Liberty: Comparing pages.

2. Cut out the title and glue it to the top of the page.

3. Cut out the passage piece. Glue it to the page below the title.

4. Cut out the flap book. Cut on the solid line to create two flaps. Apply glue to the backs of the narrow top and bottom sections and attach them to the page so the edges align horizontally.

5. Read the passage about the Liberty Bell and the Statue of Liberty. On the flaps, write what the two US symbols have in common. Under the flaps, write or draw how they are different.

Reflect on Learning

To complete the left-hand page, have students draw a Venn diagram and label one circle *Independence Day*. They may choose any other holiday to compare with Independence Day and label the other circle with the holiday name. Then, students should compare and contrast the holidays using the Venn diagram.

Give Me Liberty

The Statue of Liberty is in New York. The statue was given to America by France. It came on a boat. It had to be put together. Lady Liberty is very tall!

The Liberty Bell is in Philadelphia. It has a big crack in it! It was used to call people in for meetings. It does not ring anymore.

The Statue of Liberty and the Liberty Bell both stand for freedom.

The Liberty Bell

_____

_____

_____

_____

_____

_____

_____

_____

The Statue of Liberty

My Summer Vacation: Communities

Introduction

Review the words *rural*, *urban*, and *suburban* and discuss the definition of each term. Display pictures of each type of community. Discuss the different areas where students live. Then, assign three corners of the room as urban, suburban, and rural. Show pictures of objects (such as a tractor), housing (such as an apartment building), or landscapes (such as farmland) that would represent each community. For each picture shown, have students move to the corner of the room that would describe the community the picture illustrates.

Creating the Notebook Page

Guide students through the following steps to complete the right-hand page in their notebooks.

1. Add a Table of Contents entry for the My Summer Vacation: Communities pages.

2. Cut out the title and glue it to the top of the page.

3. Cut out the *Rural, Suburban, Urban* flap book. Cut on the solid lines to create three flaps. Apply glue to the back of the top section and attach it to the page below the title. Draw two vertical lines on the page to create three columns under the *Rural, Suburban,* and *Urban* flaps.

4. Cut out the definition cards. Read each definition. Decide whether each card describes a rural, suburban, or urban setting. Glue it under the corresponding flap.

5. Cut out the activity cards. Read each card and look at the pictures. Decide whether each card describes a rural, suburban, or urban setting. Glue each card in the correct column below the flap book.

6. On the page below the cards, write a sentence stating which setting you live in.

Reflect on Learning

To complete the left-hand page, students should draw lines to divide their pages into three sections labeled *Rural*, *Urban*, and *Suburban*. Have students draw themselves in each setting.

My Summer Vacation

Rural	Suburban	Urban
close to the city; houses and open spaces	tall buildings; many people	farmland; fewer people

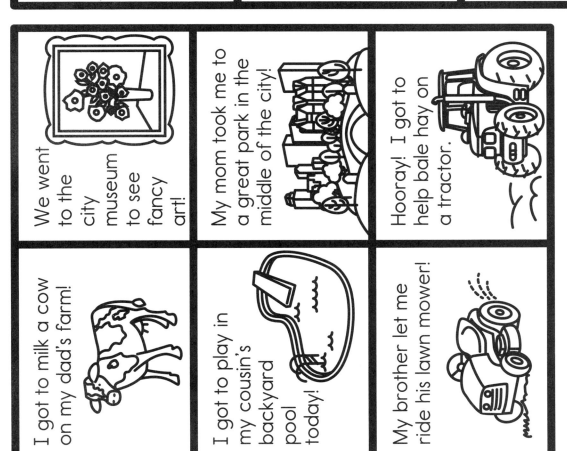

We went to the city museum to see fancy art!

My mom took me to a great park in the middle of the city!

Hooray! I got to help bale hay on a tractor.

I got to milk a cow on my dad's farm!

I got to play in my cousin's backyard pool today!

My brother let me ride his lawn mower!

Apple and Leaf Accordion Folds

Cut out the accordion pieces on the solid lines. Fold on the dashed lines, alternating the fold direction. Apply glue to the back of the last section to attach it to a notebook page.

You may modify the accordion books to have more or fewer pages by cutting off extra pages or by having students glue the first and last panels of two accordion books together.

Pumpkin Flaps

Cut out each pumpkin flap. Apply glue to the back of the narrow section to attach it to a notebook page.

Spiderweb Petal Fold

Cut out the spiderweb on the solid lines. Then, fold the flaps toward the center and back out. Apply glue to the back of the center panel to attach it to a notebook page.

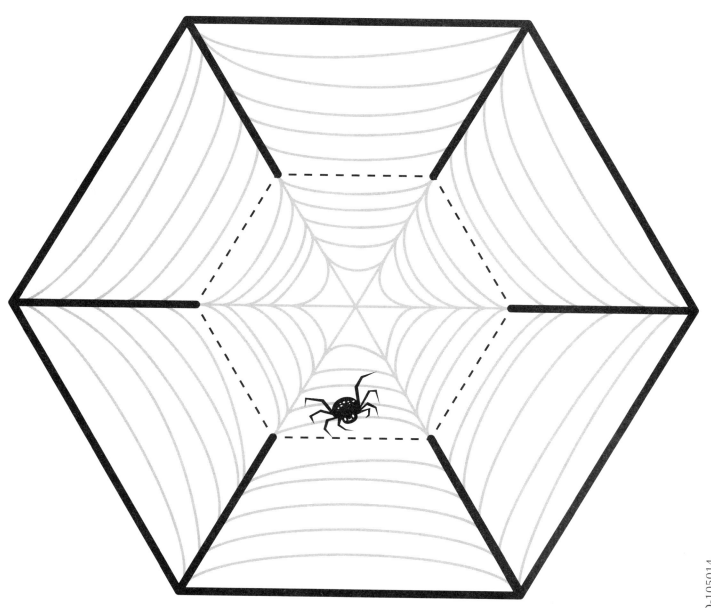

Candy Corn Flap Books

Cut out the flap books around the outside borders. Then, cut on the solid lines to create three flaps on each book. Apply glue to the backs of the left sections to attach them to a notebook page.

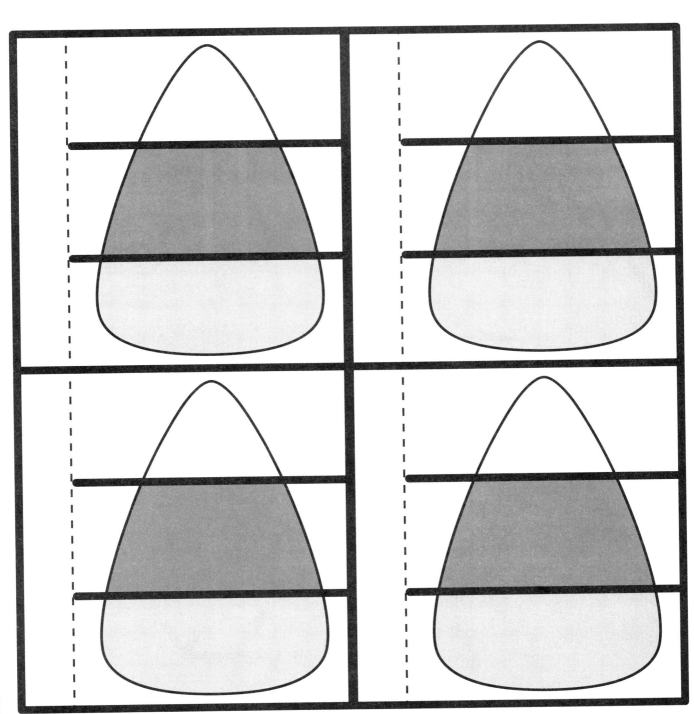

Turkey Flap Book

Cut out the flap book around the outside borders. Then, cut on the solid lines to create separate feather flaps. Apply glue to the back of the turkey body to attach it to a notebook page.

Cornucopia Pocket

Cut out the cornucopia on the solid lines. Apply glue to the backs of the six narrow sections and attach it to a notebook page. Cut out the fruit, vegetable, and plant pieces and place them in the cornucopia pocket.

Snowflake Petal Fold

Cut out the snowflake on the solid lines. Cut on the solid lines to create six flaps. Then, fold the flaps toward the center and back out. Apply glue to the back of the center panel to attach it to a notebook page.

Snowmen Flap Books

Cut out the flap books around the outside borders. Then, cut on the solid lines to create three flaps on each book. Apply glue to the backs of the left sections to attach them to a notebook page.

Tree and Ornament Flaps

Cut out the tree and glue it to a notebook page. Cut out each ornament flap. Apply glue to the back of the top section to attach it to the notebook page on and around the tree.

Fireworks Petal Folds

Cut out the fireworks on the solid lines. Cut on the solid lines to create five flaps on each firework. Then, fold the flaps toward the centers and back out. Apply glue to the backs of the center panels to attach them to a notebook page.

New Year's Eve Accordion Folds

Cut out the accordion pieces on the solid lines. Fold the left and right sides toward the center on the dashed lines, alternating the fold direction. Apply glue to the back of the left section to attach it to a notebook page.

Valentine's Day Envelope and Letters

Cut out the envelope on the solid lines. Apply glue to the backs of the three narrow sections and attach it to a notebook page. Cut out the blank letter pieces and place them in the envelope.

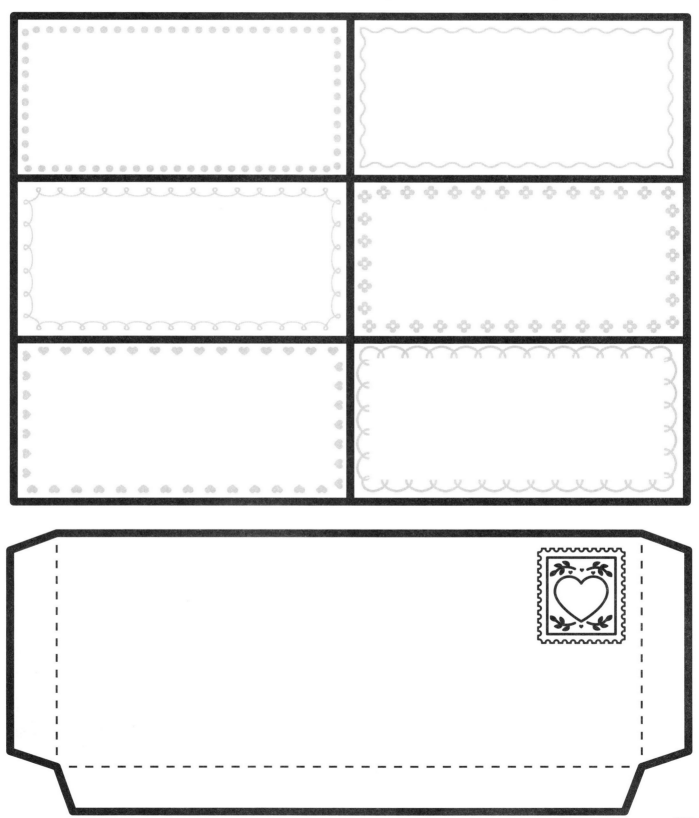

Heart Flaps

Cut out each heart flap. Apply glue to the back of the narrow section to attach it to a notebook page.

Rainbow and Pot o' Gold Flaps

Cut out the rainbow and glue it to the notebook page. Cut out each pot o' gold flap. Apply glue to the back of the narrow section to attach it to the notebook page near the rainbow.

Shamrock Flaps

Cut out each shamrock flap. Apply glue to the back of the narrow section to attach it to a notebook page.

Flower Petal Fold

Cut out the flower on the solid lines. Then, fold the flaps toward the center and back out. Apply glue to the back of the center panel to attach it to a notebook page.

Kite Flap Books

Cut out the kites and bow flap books around the outside borders. Glue the kites to a notebook page and draw a kite string for each kite. Then, apply glue to the backs of the center sections to attach the bows to the notebook page below each kite. If desired, use only one kite and any number of bows.

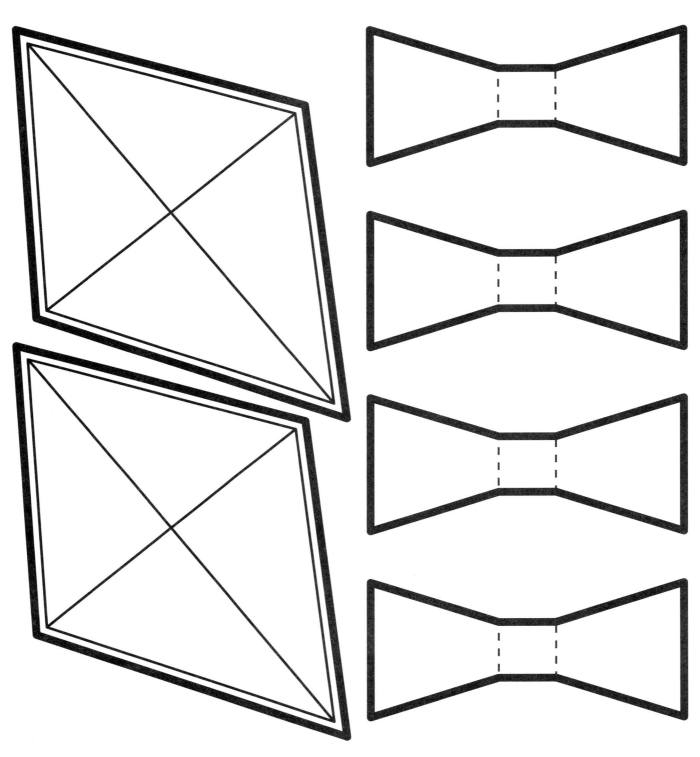

94

Nest Pockets with Eggs

Cut out the nest pockets on the solid lines. Apply glue to the backs of the three narrow sections on each pocket and attach one or both to a notebook page. Cut out the egg pieces and place them in the nest(s).

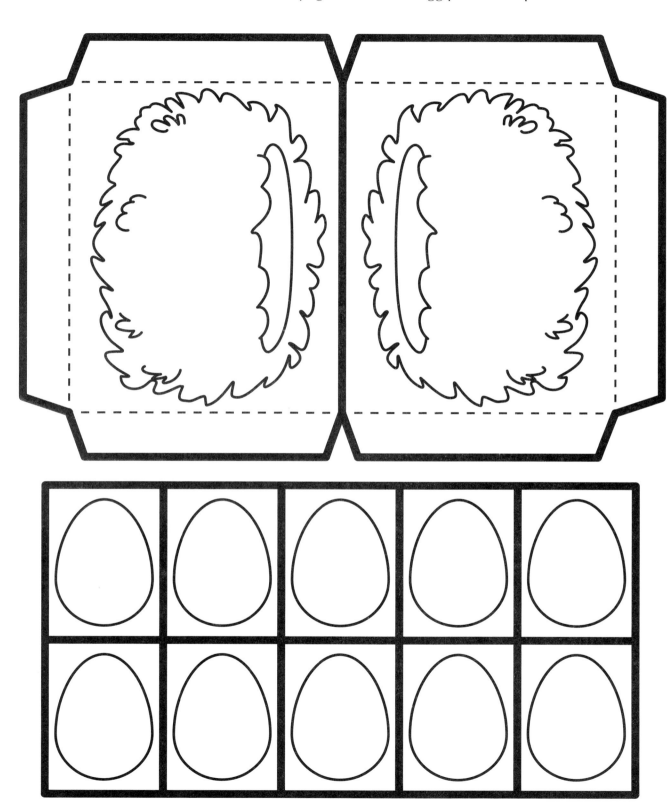

Twin Ice Pop Accordion Folds

Cut out the accordion pieces on the solid lines. Fold the left and right sides toward the center on the dashed lines, alternating the fold direction. Apply glue to the back of the center section to attach it to a notebook page.

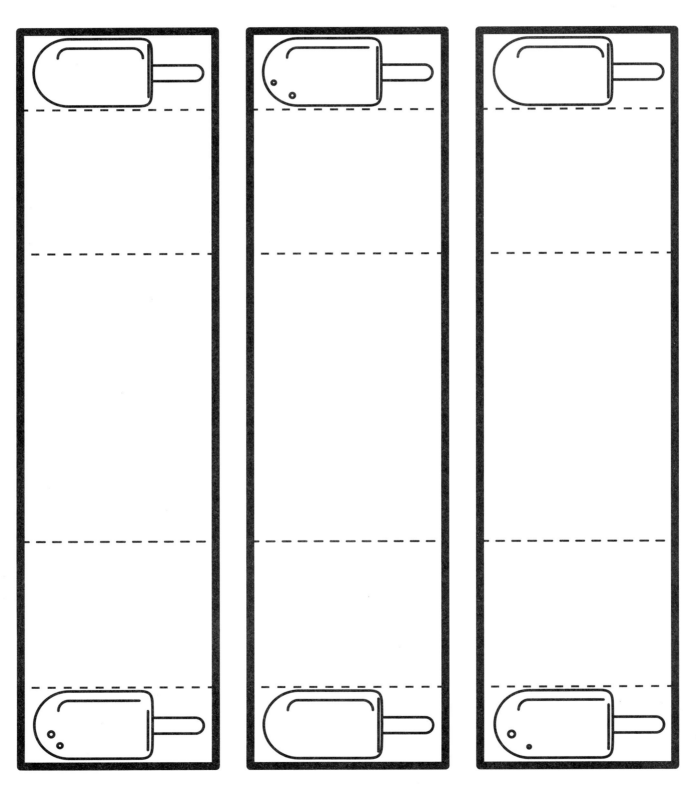